SIBERIA'S SPRITE

By the same author

The Birds of Blakeney Point

Prairie Dreams: A Human and Natural History of North America's Great Plains

Shifting Sands: Blakeney Point and the Environmental Imagination

SIBERIA'S SPRITE

A HISTORY OF FASCINATION AND DESIRE

ANDY STODDART

Pallas's Warbler (*Richard Richardson*)

Copyright © Andy Stoddart 2016. All rights reserved. No part of this publication may be reproduced, stored in a retrieval system or transmitted, in any form or by any means, electronic, mechanical, photocopying, recording or otherwise, without prior permission of the author.

ISBN - 13: 978 - 1532769030
ISBN - 10: 1532769032

Printed in the United States of America

Cover photograph: Pallas's Warbler (*Markus Varesvuo*)

I am grateful to Julian Bell, Penny Clarke, Roger Riddington and *British Birds*, Arun Singh and Markus Varesvuo for permission to reproduce photographs.

To Maja

I observed this elegant and tiny bird at the beginning of May along the Ingoda River in Dauria and although it resembles a Goldcrest it is without doubt a separate species.

Peter Simon Pallas

Frontispiece: Pallas's Warbler (*Penny Clarke*)

CONTENTS

Introduction   1
Note on nomenclature   3
1. First contact   5
2. Exiles and explorers   19
3. Imperial pursuits   29
4. Behind the wall   39
5. A European bird   51
6. What's hit is history   63
7. What's in a name?   73
8. The house on the shore   85
9. Object of desire   95
10. The art of seeing   109
11. Meanings and musings   121
12. Split decisions   131
Bibliography   143
Index of proper names   159

LIST OF PLATES

1. Peter Simon Pallas   11
2. Benedykt Dybowski   24
3. Allan Octavian Hume   33
4. Robert Swinhoe   42
5. Heinrich Gätke   55
6. Britain's first Pallas's Warbler   70
7. Henry Seebohm   77
8. Monks' House   92
9. Pallas's Warbler, Norfolk, 1958   97
10. 'Dalmatian Regulus'   110
11. Pallas's Warbler, Norfolk, 2010   125
12. Lemon-rumped Warbler   134

INTRODUCTION

The subject of this book is the Pallas's Warbler, a bird which breeds in the taiga forests of eastern Siberia and spends the winter in southern China. It lives so far away that it would barely register in the consciousness of British birdwatchers were it not for the surprising and intriguing fact that it also wanders to this country.

The memory of my first - on St. Mary's in the Isles of Scilly - is still vivid. For years the species had teased me with heart-breaking near-misses but finally, on 20th October 1985, I set eyes on my most-wanted bird. It was tiny and jewel-like, little more than a blur of stripes and flashing yellow rump, but as it danced high in a sunlit elm it was all I had hoped for and more. Since then Pallas's Warbler has come my way more than fifty times but each new encounter still brings a quickening of the pulse and a rush of joy.

I am not alone in such responses, however, for 'Siberia's sprite' has acquired amongst ornithologists and birdwatchers alike a legendary, almost mythical, status. Through a unique combination of rarity value, great aesthetic appeal and enduring scientific interest, this tiny bird has come to exercise the most remarkable hold on our collective imagination.

Nor is this a new phenomenon. For more than two centuries, from the Imperial pursuits of eighteenth century naturalists to today's taxonomic upheavals, the Pallas's Warbler has remained a constant presence and preoccupation, its story central to our ornithological history.

This book sets out to explore this history, to understand our lasting relationship with this tiny bird and its place in our fascinations and desires.

Andy Stoddart, May 2016

NOTE ON NOMENCLATURE

The now widely used name 'Pallas's Warbler' is of relatively recent invention. Its first English name, dating from the 1830s, was 'Dalmatian Regulus' though 'Pallas's Willow Warbler' became the preferred name in the second half of the nineteenth century. This was gradually replaced by 'Pallas's Leaf Warbler', still its official 'international' English name, but most refer to it simply as 'Pallas's Warbler'. Despite the small risk of confusion with the wholly unrelated Pallas's Grasshopper Warbler of the same region, this shortened form is the one in general use today. For this reason, and also to maintain consistency, this name is adopted throughout this book, even when referring to periods before it was actually in use.

FIRST CONTACT

East of the Ural Mountains lies Siberia - 'Sib Ir' or the 'Sleeping Land' to its native people. Six thousand miles from west to east, it covers a twelfth of the earth's entire land mass. This is the land of the taiga, a great forest of larch, pine and birch with, at its heart, Lake Baikal. Four hundred miles long, fifty miles wide and a mile deep, Siberia's 'Sacred Sea' contains within its cold, clear depths a fifth of the planet's fresh water.

These waters feed the Angara, a tributary of the mighty Yenisei which, like Siberia's other great rivers the Ob and the Lena, flows north to the Arctic Ocean. Beyond Lake Baikal, however, in the region known as 'Transbaikalia', the rivers join to form the Amur, whose waters flow east - to the Pacific.

The upper headwaters of the Amur - the 'Black Dragon River' - were acquired by Russia in the seventeenth century. With the accession in 1613 of Michael I, first of the Romanovs, Russia's push to the east gathered pace. The town of Yeniseysk, on the Yenisei, was founded in 1619 with Krasnoyarsk, higher upriver, in 1628 and Irkutsk, just west of Lake Baikal, in 1652. Transbaikalia was then settled quickly, with Chita established in 1653 and Nerchinsk the following year. Control of the region was, however, contested with the Manchu rulers of China, a dispute only resolved in the 1689 Treaty of Nerchinsk which was to fix the two countries' borders for nearly two centuries. Under its terms Russia gave up its ambitions over the Lower Amur but retained control of Transbaikalia.

For most European Russians, however, Siberia remained a great empty space, a white void on the map onto which any vision could be projected. For many it represented Russia's virgin state, a rural idyll where the nation's original purity and innocence could still be found. Others had a more practical vision, imagining it as a place where anything undesirable could be safely banished. One of Siberia's earliest functions was to receive society's unwanted, the criminal and the dissident, sent there in the certain knowledge that, even if they survived the two-year journey, they would never return. More intellectual or scientific engagements with Siberia were therefore slow to develop. Those who went there were expected to labour in the mines, not to send back reports on the flora and fauna.

Nevertheless, the eighteenth century saw the first stirrings of scientific curiosity about this new frontier. In 1720-28, at the behest of Peter the Great, the German botanist Daniel Messerschmidt travelled to the Baikal region to 'collect rarities and medicinal plants'. Shortly afterwards, in 1733, the German naturalist and geographer Johann Gmelin was invited to travel with Vitus Bering's 'Second Kamchatka Expedition'. (Bering's first expedition, in 1726-30, had charted some of the waters around Imperial Russia's new Far East but much of the region, particularly the stretch of water between Russia and America, remained unknown).

The academic component of the second expedition, of which Gmelin formed part, left St. Petersburg in August 1733, crossing the Yenisei at Yeniseysk and reaching Irkutsk in March 1735. On his arrival Gmelin began to collect plant specimens around Lake Baikal, travelling to Argun (on its northern shore) and also to Kyakhta, a border trading town where the Selenga River crosses from Mongolia.

Gmelin's part of the expedition joined Bering and his men at Yakutsk (on the Lena to the north-east of Lake Baikal) in September 1736, intending to travel on with them to Kamchatka. However, a fire here destroyed Gmelin's accommodation and all his specimens and notes, and the subsequent summer was spent retracing his steps and attempting to replace his losses. Gmelin eventually decided to return to St. Petersburg, meeting in Yeniseysk in January 1739 the German naturalist Georg Steller. Gmelin promptly recommended that Steller take his place in the planned exploration of Kamchatka though he required little persuasion. On hearing of Bering's second expedition, Steller had left St. Petersburg in 1738 and, spurred no doubt by his meeting with Gmelin, caught up with Bering at Okhotsk, on the Pacific coast, in March 1740.

The expedition was ill-fated, however. Storm-driven and suffering from scurvy, Bering died on an uninhabited island (later called 'Bering Island') in the Commander Islands group off Kamchatka in December 1741. Steller survived, reaching the Russian mainland, but died in 1746 at Tyumen, just east of the Urals, during his return to St. Petersburg.

The expedition is most famous for its landfall at Kayak Island, Alaska on 20th July 1741 and for Steller's discovery there of a dark species of jay which today bears his name. He also made other important discoveries along the Pacific coast, including what are today known as Steller's Eider and Steller's

Sea Eagle, but left little record of his passage through the Siberian hinterland. This task was to fall to Gmelin who, on his return, published *Reise durch Sibirien von dem Jahr 1733 bis 1743* and his great botanical work *Flora Sibirica sive Historia plantarum Sibiriae*. This latter publication, based on his observations and collections, contains descriptions of over a thousand plant species with illustrations of almost three hundred.

It would be twenty-five years before another European naturalist set foot in Siberia but the next to do so would also be a German. Peter Simon Pallas was born on 22nd September 1741, the son of a Berlin surgeon. He became interested in natural history before the age of fifteen and at nineteen received a doctor's degree (on the subject of intestinal worms) from the University of Leiden. He subsequently travelled widely in England and Holland, visiting their natural history collections, and in 1766 published his first scientific work, *Miscellanea Zoologica*, before going on to publish *Spicilegia Zoologica*, a new system for the classification of animals.

This was an exciting time to be a naturalist. The Enlightenment of the eighteenth century was an intellectual revolution, heralding a bold new era of scientific discipline and enquiry. Botany was the earliest branch of natural history to flourish, followed by entomology and geology, but soon all its aspects were the subject of active enquiry, and ornithology became a serious area of study in its own right. In Britain this new knowledge was enshrined in works such as Thomas Pennant's 1761-76 *British Zoology* and John Latham's 1787 *General Synopsis of Birds* but naturalists were active across Europe too, with Mathurin Brisson publishing his influential *Ornithologie* in 1760.

Pallas corresponded widely, gaining rapid recognition from Europe's scientific community, and was granted membership of the Royal Society of London at the age of twenty-three. Amongst his correspondents was Pennant whom he met in Holland in 1765. Pennant was a particularly useful contact whose network extended not just to the 'parson-naturalist' Gilbert White of Selborne but also to international scientific luminaries such as Carl Linnaeus and the Comte de Buffon.

Pallas's contact with this Europe-wide intellectual elite and his growing reputation as a naturalist inevitably brought him to the attention of Catherine II of Russia. From the moment of seizing power in 1762, Catherine began to expand Russia's dominions, promote its economic development, overhaul the country's administrative structures and pursue policies of Westernisation. She also sought to enhance Russia's position on the world stage and establish it as the intellectual and cultural equal of the rest of Europe. Missing no opportunity to advance this cause, she assiduously cultivated the French philosopher Voltaire, and in this context her interest in the young Pallas is of little surprise.

Catherine invited Pallas to St. Petersburg in 1767. Here he was appointed Professor of Natural History at the Imperial Academy of Sciences, a post vacant for two decades but previously occupied by both Steller and Gmelin. However, his stay in the city was to be brief.

The new Empress was intent on mapping and documenting her expanding Empire and its resources - its geography, its people and also its natural history - and supported the Academy in its plans to survey the country's vast hinterland. These 'Academy Expeditions' were intended, in Catherine's words, to 'put in proper light the condition and the products of [our] hitherto unknown provinces.' Though intended primarily to advance scientific knowledge, the expeditions were of course also inextricably linked with Catherine's economic and political motives.

The expeditions were an irresistible attraction to Pallas. Foreign travel was, for most, difficult and expensive, the preserve of the wealthy or at least those with good connections and a rich or powerful patron. Catherine's backing therefore provided the perfect opportunity for exploration.

First to leave St. Petersburg were the naturalists Johann Güldenstädt (to the Caucasus) and Ivan Lepechin (to the Lower Volga and Caspian region). Pallas left the capital in June 1768 accompanied by Samuel Gmelin (nephew of Johann), initially to the south - to Samara on the Lower Volga - but then east, crossing the Urals to Tobolsk on the West Siberian Plain. He arrived in Krasnoyarsk, on the Yenisei, on 10th October 1771, travelling from there by way of the Altai Mountains to Lake Baikal and beyond.

Throughout the journey he sent reports back to St. Petersburg. These form a travelogue, a narrative account of the land, its people and, of course, its natural history. They were not intended for immediate publication but, as Pallas makes clear, events took a different course:

> By the plan first designed, the natural curiosity of the public would not have been gratified, it being proposed not to publish any part of this tour till the return of the gentlemen engaged in it: but, that love of science, which is one of the great ornaments of Count Orlow, director of the academy, induced him to gratify the literary world, by forwarding the publication of these travels.

Pallas's reports were published as *Reise durch verschiedene Provinzen des Russischen Reichs* (1771-76), subsequently translated into French and also into a truncated English version. This latter translation was published as *Travels into Siberia and*

Plate 1. Peter Simon Pallas

Tartary, provinces of the Russian empire, and comprised Volumes II-IV of Rev. Dr. John Trusler's 1788-89 *The habitable world described*, the account of the Siberian part of Pallas's journey appearing in Volume IV. His journal for 1772 describes the approach to Irkutsk:

> There being nothing now to prevent my prosecuting my intended journey, into the eastern parts of Siberia, and my health being restored, I set out, on the 7th of March, from Krasnojarsk, on my road to Irkuzkaja, a distance of 544 miles; where I removed on the 14th of March. This road is tolerably passable; sometimes we travelled on sledges, and sometimes on waggons. Post-stations are here erected, at proper distances, with horses, and good warm and white, painted rooms, for the reception of travellers; and the country is all along inhabited by Siberians, or Russian colonists.

Although written as a travelogue rather than a detailed natural history, Pallas's diaries nevertheless made frequent reference to birds:

> On account of the warm weather, we saw now, about Irkuzkaja, the last passage of the snow-larks (*Alauda alpestris*) [Shore Larks], and black sparrows (*Fringilla flavirostris*) [Twite]; and there was also arriving, a kind of parti-coloured jackdaw, which spends the winter in China, or the warmer part of the states of the Mogul (*Corvus Dauricus*) [Daurian Jackdaw].

Early spring 1772 continued to be mild:

> On my arrival at Selenginskaja [on 10th April], the river Selenga was almost free from ice; but it shut up the Tschikoi and Chilok, which last river was not open till the 20th of April. The sun, however, was so warm, as to cover with green and bloom the heights situated in the south. On the 13th of April we saw the first wind-flowers (*anemone pulsatilla*), which sprung abundantly from the sand, and increased amazingly.

However, the weather was not to last:

> On May the 5th, at day-break, a great deal of wet snow fell, which, with the stony and miry roads, made our way almost impassable, and extremely toilsome... With the greatest pain, however, and loss of time, we passed the Uda, and crept over

another mountain, covered with larches; and late in the afternoon found ourselves at the distance only of twelve miles from the place we left at break of day. We were fortunate, however, to meet here with a deserted winter-hut, with a stove, but without roof, door, or window, where we slept, and were sheltered from the snow. Next morning, after a chilling night, our desert-habitation looked like a field of battle. Near it stood our horses and waggons, of which we had 20, but 11 of them having died in the night, with the frost and hunger, lay stretched out on the snow, and had attracted all the crows and ravens of the forest, whose cawings rendered the place still more dreadful.

There were, however, ornithological compensations. At the time specimens represented the only way to identify or study birds, so collecting was the main preoccupation:

In our wretchedness, however, the birds of the forest, which, stimulated by hunger, gathered about our hut, gave me no little pleasure. We threw rubbish out of the hut, which still further decoyed them, so that we could shoot a great number of rare birds through the window-holes. Here I got seven, new species of unknown birds, some of which I never could meet with afterwards, as they inhabit the innermost and thickest part of the forest, and are very shy. These were, *Turdus ruficollis, & Alpinus, Motacilla Cyanura, Emheriza minuta, rustica, Chrysocilla et Spodocephala.* Towards night we found several, little birds in the snow, killed by hunger and the frost, and a little species of blue-tailed hedge-sparrow (*Motac. Cyanurus*) which, though extremely shy, flew into our hut for shelter, and hopped boldly about.

This was clearly a 'fall' of birds, stalled by the adverse weather during their migration from winter quarters in southern China to breeding grounds in Siberia. We can easily identify most of those in Pallas's list: Red-throated Thrush, Red-flanked

Bluetail and Little, Rustic, Yellow-browed and Black-faced Buntings. All are typical migrants to the region in spring.

On 9th May Pallas crossed into the Amur watershed:

> We reached the bottom of the partition mountain, which divides Dauria from Siberia. This mountain rises gradually with a gentle ascent, till we come to that steep, rocky part, which, by the name of Jableni-Daba, separates the brooks of the Baikal and Lena from those of the Amur.

Two days later, on 11th May, Pallas reached the Ingoda River, long claimed by Russia as the source of the Amur though in reality the honour belongs to the Onon, rising in Mongolia's Khentii Mountains. The Ingoda rises in the Yablonoi Mountains, near the Mongolian border, and twists for four hundred miles through forested hills before passing through Chita and joining the Onon. Now renamed the Shilka, it joins the Argun, their waters combining to become the Amur.

Here on the Ingoda Pallas notes improving conditions: 'On the warmer mountains about the Ingoda, the larch-trees began to put out their leaves; the birches were dropping their juice, and the *Rhododendrum Dauricum* shewed its purple bloom'. He was greatly impressed with the biological richness of the region, indeed for a scientist his journal sometimes verges on the rhapsodic:

> None can conceive a more magnificent sight than the woods and steep mountains along the Onon, whose southern side was enamelled with the peach-coloured bloom of the wild, Siberian apricot; and its north side with the deep-purple blossoms of the *Rhododendrum Dauricum.* Through my whole travels I never saw so romantic a region.

Nevertheless, despite such delights, Pallas suffered greatly on his journey, succumbing not just to the hardships of constant travel and the rigours of the Siberian weather but also to a creeping melancholy and hypochondria. He returned to St. Petersburg on 30th July 1774 with, in his own words, 'an infirm body and a hoary head', his exertions having left him prematurely grey. He had, however, brought back a host of valuable specimens for the city's Kunstammer Museum, making an extraordinary and pioneering contribution to Siberian natural history, in particular its ornithology.

Pallas remained in St. Petersburg for almost twenty years, enjoying a comfortable and privileged life as a favourite of Catherine. Here he began to pull together his notes and continued to correspond, including to Pennant who used much of his material in his 1784-85 *Arctic Zoology*, but in 1793-94 Pallas led a second expedition, this time to the Black Sea. On his return he was rewarded by Catherine with a property in the Crimea to which he retired in 1796 and where he continued to document the scientific discoveries of his own and his contemporaries' expeditions.

Amongst these publications were accounts of Güldenstädt's travels in the Caucasus and of his own expedition to Crimea. He also completed a major botanical review - *Flora Rossica* - but his greatest work was *Zoographia Rosso-Asiatica*, based on his collections and observations in Siberia and containing a full account of the species recorded on the expedition.

Pallas took the by then unorthodox step of writing his masterpiece in Latin. At a time when other European academies were moving increasingly towards publication in their own language, the Academy of Sciences remained committed to Latin as the international scientific language, not changing to Russian until the mid-nineteenth century. The process of writing and publishing was long and tortuous, however. Pallas worked on the manuscript for fifteen years, completing it in 1807, but due to delays over the engraving of the accompanying plates the *Zoographia* remained unpublished at the time of his death - in his birthplace of Berlin - on 8th September 1811.

Zoographia Rosso-Asiatica was finally published (without the plates) in 1826 and then in a fully illustrated edition in 1831. Only now could the full extent of Pallas's work be appreciated. Amongst the species described by the author himself and still associated with him through their English name are Pallas's Cormorant (now extinct), Pallas's Fish Eagle, Pallas's Gull, Pallas's Sandgrouse, Pallas's Grasshopper Warbler and Pallas's Rosefinch. Named after him (and described by others) are Pallas's Dipper and Pallas's Reed Bunting.

Also contained in the *Zoographia* is a formal scientific description of one of Pallas's most celebrated discoveries, a tiny warbler which he had collected on the Ingoda River in May 1772 and which was completely unfamiliar not only to Pallas but also to science. Given the scientific name '*Motacilla proregulus*', its entry in the *Zoographia* begins as follows:

> *Hanc elegantissimam et minutissimam inter nostrates aviculam initio Maji ad Ingodam fl. Dauriae observavi, et licet Regulo simillima sit, distinctam tamen esse specie, minime dubito* [I observed this elegant and tiny bird at the beginning of May along the Ingoda River in Dauria and although it resembles a Goldcrest it is without doubt a separate species].

This was followed by its first published description:

> *Magnitudo et facies omnino Reguli. Rostrum superius nigram, maxilla inferior lutescente; apice fusca. Plumulae supra nares citreo-flavae, atque hinc continuator laeniola utrinque supraciliaris ajusdem, coloris quae continuator versus occiput linea subinterrupta alba, et compare connectitor. Vertex intermedius fusco-virescens, linea longitudinali flavescente, versus nucham*

albida. Punctum fuscum ante oculos et striga fusca ab oculis ad nucham. Dorsum cinereo-flavum vel virescens, ut et tetrices caudae; sed Zona lata uropygii albido-flava. Subtus avicula alba, genicalis pedum flavescentibus. Alae fuscae; remiges 17 limbo exteriore flavae, interior albae; prima minima; tectrices secondariae earumque incumbents flavescenti-albae, unde striga duplex alarum. Humeri subtus albi, margine flavo. Cauda subbifurca fusca; rectrices acuminatae, oris exterioribus flavescentibus. Pondus drachmae 1. Cum scrupulo. Mensuro a rostri apice ad uropygium 2". 1"'. caudae 1". 7"'. alarum expansarum 5". 7"'. ulnae 1". 10"'.

Here, albeit in Latin, was a complete and systematic description of the specimen, setting out the full complexities of its plumage: its dusky eyestripes, yellow supercilia, dark crown with pale central stripe, green upperparts, pale double wing-bars and yellow rump. Included also are the colours of the bare parts (the bill and legs), some 'wing formula' details (the relative lengths of the primary feathers) and a series of measurements, including its weight.

The existence and appearance of what would later become known as Pallas's Warbler were now a matter of record. Little else, however, was known about the species. It had emerged, blinking, into the light of scientific recognition but the story of this tiny bird remained almost completely untold.

EXILES AND EXPLORERS

Ornithology developed rapidly in the nineteenth century and, with Western Empires continuing to expand, there were ever greater opportunities to travel to distant parts of the world in search of specimens.

These opportunities were facilitated in part by improvements in transport and communication but just as important was the introduction in the 1850s of breech-loading double-barrelled shotguns and fine shot cartridges. These meant that it was now possible to shoot small birds without obliterating them entirely and also to shoot them in flight. The specimen collector was therefore increasingly well equipped and, inevitably, the pace of collecting and the discovery of new species accelerated.

New taxidermy techniques were also available. Most notably, the introduction of arsenic soap meant that skins could be kept permanently. This new availability of durable reference material greatly aided the work of the museum scientists and their authority grew. Museums became the source of all ornithological knowledge and their Curators the acknowledged experts, publishing not just books, catalogues and avifaunas but also a proliferation of papers in an ever-growing number of scientific journals. Avian classification and distribution were their main preoccupations, most publications comprising lists of species collected from a particular area or descriptions of species new to science.

However, while ornithology developed rapidly in Europe, the death of Catherine II in 1796 brought a premature end to Russian explorations. The reigns of Paul I and Alexander I were far less supportive of natural history study, and by 1812 the nation's attention was focused more on defeating Napoleon than on collecting birds.

After 1825, however, ornithology received a new impetus under Nicholas I. A key architect of this resurgence was the German Johann Brandt who in 1831 took up post as Director of the Zoological Museum at the Academy of Sciences in St. Petersburg. With his support, naturalists began to venture once more to the far reaches of the Empire.

By now Russia was extending its influence into the Lower Amur region and in 1854 east Siberia's Governor-general Nikolai Muraviev mounted a great land grab of Chinese territory, annexing an area the size of France and Germany combined. Onto this new frontier were projected dreams of mineral riches and national renewal. Fed by reports from the New World of the California goldrush and the great westward migration, the Amur was envisioned as Russia's route to a new greatness as a Pacific as well as a European power. The annexation was legitimised in the 1858 Treaty of Aigun, effectively reversing the Treaty of Nerchinsk and transferring from China to Russia over 200,000 square miles between the Stanovoy Mountains and the Amur. A whole new region beyond the Ingoda River was now open for exploration.

Naturalists were active in the region even before the Treaty was signed. Amongst the first was the ornithologist Alexander von Middendorff, Assistant Professor of Zoology at Kiev University. Between 1843 and 1845 Middendorff travelled on behalf of the Academy of Sciences to the Taymyr Peninsula, eventually reaching the (still Chinese) Lower Amur by way of the Sea of Okhotsk. He sent many specimens back to St. Petersburg and subsequently published an account of his journey, *Reise in den äußersten Norden und Osten Sibiriens*, the ornithological content being contained in the 'Zoology' sections published in 1853.

Amongst the specimens obtained on the Lower Amur was one he termed '*Sylvia* (*Phyllopneuste*) *proregulus*', the same tiny warbler which Pallas had collected on the Ingoda in 1772, here noted as a summer visitor to the region, arriving in May. Unfortunately, Middendorff did not draw a distinction between Pallas's Warbler and its close relative the Yellow-browed Warbler, the latter only just (in 1842) described from India. However, the identification as Pallas's Warbler of two Middendorff specimens from the south side of the Stanovoy Mountains - one from Markul on 18th June 1844, the other from the Salurnai River on 3rd July the same year - is certain. Middendorff is today commemorated in the English name of Middendorff's Grasshopper Warbler, a species of warbler in the genus *Locustella* breeding around the Sea of Okhotsk.

Ten years later, Gustav Radde, a native of West Prussia but latterly Curator of the Caucasian Museum and Library in Tbilisi, travelled as botanist on the astronomer Ludwig Schwarz's 1855 'East Siberian Expedition' for the Russian Geographical Society, its goal to reach Kamchatka and 'Russian America' (as Alaska was then known). On his return he published in 1862-63 his experiences in *Reisen im Süden von Ost-Sibirien in den Jahren 1855-59*.

Radde was not just a botanist, however, and avidly collected insect and bird specimens, many of which were sent back to St. Petersburg. Amongst the latter, he found Pallas's Warbler in east Transbaikalia, collecting an example at the settlement of Kullussutajevsk - near Lake Tarei Nor - on 5th September 1856. Shortly afterwards, he discovered there another Siberian leaf-warbler, now known as Radde's Warbler, whose specific name - *schwarzi* - recognises that of his travelling companion.

To the south of the Lower Amur lies the Ussuri region, sandwiched between the Ussuri River and the Pacific. Here a more southern flora and fauna are evident and the forests are very different in character. In place of the endless larches, pines and birches of the taiga zone can be found a greater variety of temperate tree species - oaks, hornbeams, limes and maples - with conifers confined to the higher slopes. Here the dark uniformity of Siberia fades, and the forests are home to bright southern flycatchers and butterflies. The Russian botanist Karl Maximovicz was the first to confirm that Pallas's Warbler occurred here also, obtaining a specimen at Stanitza Busse on the Ussuri in 1855 while exploring the region on behalf of the Academy of Sciences with the Russo-German zoologist and geographer Leopold von Schrenck.

Most prominent amongst this generation of Siberian explorers were three exiled Polish zoologists: Wiktor Godlewski, Michael Jankowski and Benedykt Dybowski. In 1863 Poland still formed part of the Russian Empire and, following the ill-fated 'January Uprising' of that year against czarist domination, tens of thousands were arrested and either executed or exiled.

Siberia was by now well established as a place for banishing the unwanted, and Transbaikalia was a common destination. Chita had already become the final resting place for the ill-fated 'Decembrists', survivors of an inept coup attempt against Nicholas I in December 1825. These were the first Russian prisoners of conscience, exiled for political reasons, to enter the 'katorga' system of penal labour, the forerunner of the infamous Gulags.

In the wake of the 1863 uprising a new wave of Polish political exiles, known as 'Sybiraks', was sent to Transbaikalia, amongst them Godlewski, Jankowski and Dybowski. They arrived in Siberia in 1864 but were eventually released from their sentences of hard labour and allowed to resume their zoological studies. This was at least partly due to support from Poland in the form of Wladislaw Taczanowski, Conservator of the Zoological Museum in Warsaw, to whom they wrote regularly and sent consignments of bird specimens.

All three exiles worked together in studying the fauna of the region, Godlewski and Dybowski collecting two male examples of a bunting at Kultuk, at the south-west corner of Lake Baikal. On reaching Warsaw, these were described by Taczanowski in 1874 as a new species - 'Godlewski's Bunting'. Godlewski was to spend his whole period of exile in the Baikal area, eventually leaving Siberia in 1877.

Jankowski left his companions in 1874, settling for five years on Askold Island, in Peter the Great Bay east of Vladivostok. Here he observed Pallas's Warbler amongst the island's many migrant birds. Later he moved to Sedimi, west of Vladivostok, remaining there from 1882 to 1887, and also collected birds in neighbouring Korea. It was in March 1886, during his time at Sedimi, that Jankowski also collected an unfamiliar bunting. This too was sent to Taczanowski who, in

Plate 2. Benedykt Dybowski

1888, named it 'Jankowski's Bunting', today an extremely localised and highly threatened species.

Though destined never to have a new bunting named after him, Dybowski was eventually the most travelled of the three. He was also the most published, contributing to a number of European journals, and made perhaps the greatest contribution to our knowledge of Siberian birds. He was initially held at Irkutsk, Chita and Darasun (about forty miles south-east of Chita on the Ingoda River) but after being released from his sentence in 1866 he settled in Kultuk and took up duties as a doctor.

Taczanowski published some of Dybowski's early observations in 1872 in a paper in *Journal für Ornithologie* entitled 'Bericht über die ornithologischen Untersuchungen des Dr. Dybowski in Ost-Sibirien'. Here we read that Dybowski found Pallas's Warbler, here called '*Reguloides proregulus*', to be relatively common at Kultuk and in the wider Baikal region, arriving at the beginning of June and inhabiting the hillside birch and mixed woods as high as the tree line. Throughout this region its song could be heard, described as 'varied and sweet, and so loud that it rings through the forest, and it is astonishing as coming from so small [a] bird.' Although there was no evidence of it breeding at Kultuk, he found nests at Petrovsk, east of Lake Baikal on the left bank of the Selenga River:

> The nests were placed on young Pines or old moss-covered Cedars [Siberian Stone Pine] on the branches near the stem, three to four metres high, and were neatly constructed of fine grass-bents and green moss, oven-shaped, the opening being towards the trunk of the tree, and lined with feathers and horse or cattle hair.

'In autumn', he notes, 'the birds form flocks, flying from tree to tree together with flocks of tits. They stay until mid-September, with a few stragglers remaining until 25th.' He also recorded the species further to the east at Darasun mineral springs and at the frontier station of Alt-Tsuruchaitui on the Argun River.

Dybowski's travels also took him well beyond Transbaikalia. Leaving his compatriots in Kultuk in 1869, he took part in the latter stages of Ivan Skolkov's expedition to the Lower Amur, Sakhalin and the Ussuri and Vladivostok region. Guiding them was the Russian explorer Nikolai Przewalski, here on his first major expedition. Przewalski noted Pallas's Warblers arriving along the Ussuri between the end of March and the end of April. They were particularly common around Lake Khanka. One of his specimens from this location was sent to St. Petersburg and subsequently listed by its Curator Theodor Pleske in his 1889-92 *Ornithographia Rossica*.

Between 1872 and 1874 Dybowski undertook further travels in the Lower Amur and Ussuri region as far as Vladivostok, Askold Island and the nearby town of Bolshoy Kamen. By 1878 he was back in Europe, finally allowed home, only to travel once more to Vladivostok, Kamchatka and the Commander Islands the following year, returning finally to Europe in 1883.

Subsequent published observations of Pallas's Warbler include those of the Russian naturalist Schwedow who observed good numbers on 20th and 25th August 1881 in the public gardens of Irkutsk and along the Uschakovka River about twenty-five miles from the town. Also in the Baikal region, it was noted on 18th August 1885 on migration near Kyakhta by the resident naturalist, and later Museum Curator, Wladislaw Molleson. In the Ussuri region the brothers Friedrich and Heinrich Dörries observed the species on 18th September 1882 at the station of Baranovskij on the Razdolnaya (Suifen) River between Ussuriysk and Vladivostok. They also noted it, as had Jankowski, on Askold Island.

By the end of the 1880s the breeding range and status of Pallas's Warbler in Russia had been largely revealed. It was apparently absent in western and northern Siberia (it was, for example, not recorded on the British ornithologist Henry Seebohm's 1877 expedition to the lower reaches of the Yenisei) but it appeared to be common around Lake Baikal and the Upper and Central Lena and Vitim Rivers, thence eastward through Transbaikalia to the Stanovoy Mountains, the Lower Amur and the Ussuri region as far as the Pacific coast and Sakhalin. It arrived in the more southerly parts of the Ussuri region in late March, peaked there in April and reached the Lower Amur in May and the Baikal region at the beginning of June. It could be seen on autumn migration around Lake Baikal from mid-August and had left the region by late September.

There were, however, many other things still to discover about this species. Did it breed anywhere else? Where did it winter? Where did it pass through on migration? The answers to these questions would have to be sought outside Russia.

IMPERIAL PURSUITS

The other great Asian theatre of Imperial expansion was India. After 1757 much of the subcontinent found itself under the control of the British East India Company and, following the Indian Rebellion of 1857, under direct British rule. It became not just the jewel in the crown of Britain's expanding Empire but a happy ornithological hunting ground for a privileged class of British soldiers, administrators and political officers.

Amongst the latter was the British naturalist Brian Hodgson. Sailing to India in 1818, Hodgson initially took up a position with the East India Company in Calcutta but ill health brought a move to Kumaon (in today's state of Uttarakhand) and then to Kathmandu where in 1820 he became Assistant Resident to the Court of Nepal. In 1833 he was promoted to Resident and remained in Kathmandu for another twelve years, retiring in 1845 to Darjeeling and returning to Britain in 1858.

Prior to Hodgson's arrival in Nepal few Western naturalists had made any investigations in the country. It therefore presented enormous opportunities for exploration and discovery. Hodgson took a special interest in its birds but he was not permitted to travel beyond the Kathmandu Valley and was restricted in his contacts with Nepalese society. Nevertheless, he collected avidly in the Valley and along the route south to the Indian border (and also engaged Nepalese hunters to bring him birds), eventually amassing over 9,500 bird specimens of over 650 species, of which more than 120 were new to science. He also trained a number of native artists to produce coloured drawings to accompany his specimens.

He published more than sixty papers on birds, mainly between 1829 and 1847. Most appeared in the *Journal of the Asiatic Society of Bengal* but he also published in the *Proceedings of the Zoological Society of London*, *Asiatic Researches* and the *Calcutta Journal of Natural History*. Hodgson lacked formal scientific training, however, and was prone to errors in his draft publications. In particular, he was untutored in writing plumage descriptions and in the emerging conventions of scientific nomenclature, and he received less than overwhelming support for his efforts from the ornithological establishment, both in India and in Britain.

His relationships with the *Journal of the Asiatic Society* and its Editor were particularly fraught. For example, his 1843 'Catalogue of Nepalese birds presented to the Asiatic Society, duly named and classified by the Donor (and revised by the Society's Curator)' was, as is made clear in its title, extensively amended by Edward Blyth, the Society's Museum Curator from 1841 to 1862, and emerged in a confused and unsatisfactory state. (Blyth himself was an important figure in Indian ornithology, describing a number of the small leaf warblers including Yellow-browed Warbler, Orange-barred Leaf Warbler and Ashy-throated Leaf Warbler though today he is most widely remembered in the English names for Blyth's Pipit and Blyth's Reed Warbler).

Hodgson sent specimens to a number of museums including the Zoological Society of London (until 1850 housing an important collection), the East India Company Museum and the Natural History Department of the British Museum. A large consignment of 2,596 skins, together with drawings and an accompanying index, was sent to the latter institution where its Keeper of Zoology, John Gray, and his brother, George Gray - the Museum's ornithological assistant - were given the task of examining them and, at Hodgson's request, drawing up a catalogue. John Gray had been appointed in 1840 to improve the museum's curatorial practices and, having embarked on a major collection-building programme, would have greatly welcomed Hodgson's Nepalese specimens.

Hodgson's relations with the Grays were also difficult, however. They failed to take proper care of his specimens, removed many of his labels, made errors in documentation and attributed a number of new species not to Hodgson but to others, including Blyth and the ornithological publisher John Gould. Ultimately Hodgson was only credited with 79 of his new bird discoveries. Such events did little to endear museum naturalists to Hodgson and he remained bitter about their position of power in ornithology. In the words of his first biographer, William Hunter, his collection represented 'a vast quarry, out of which scholars surreptitiously build their own fame.'

Hodgson's failure, despite repeated attempts, to publish a major work on Himalayan birds also obscured his achievements. Nevertheless, his chief legacy - his collection, published papers, unpublished notes and drawings - still exists, and his contribution to our first understandings of Nepal's birds remains unsurpassed. Today he is most remembered in the English names of Hodgson's Bushchat and Hodgson's Redstart but just as significant perhaps was the presence in his skin collection of a small warbler which closely resembled that described by Pallas from Siberia.

It too was tiny and Goldcrest-like with bold supercilia, a pronounced pale central crown-stripe, double wing-bars and a prominent and well-defined pale yellow rump patch. It was formally described by the Grays as '*Abrornis chloronotus*' and published in their 1847 *Catalogue of the specimens and drawings of Mammalia and Birds of Nepal and Thibet presented by B.H. Hodgson Esq., to the British Museum* (a second Catalogue was published in 1863).

The existence in the Himalayas of Hodgson's warbler was then duly noted in a series of major publications on India's birds. The first of these was by the British naturalist Thomas Jerdon, known today through the English names of, for example, Jerdon's Courser and Jerdon's Bushchat.

Arriving in India in 1836 as a surgeon with the East India Company, Jerdon quickly set about collecting birds in Kashmir, at the Indian hill stations, in the Khasi Hills and in Assam, publishing in 1862-64 *The Birds of India,* detailing the occurrence of over a thousand species and including notes on their habits and a number of field sketches. Amongst those listed was Hodgson's warbler from Nepal's Kathmandu Valley to which he ascribed the scientific name '*Reguloides chloronotus*'. Its distribution was given as 'the Himalayas from Mussooree [Mussoorie] to Bootan [Bhutan]; also in Burmah, China, and the Dehra Doon [Dehradun].'

The leader of the next generation of Indian ornithologists was Allan Octavian Hume. Arriving in India in 1849 to pursue a

Plate 3. Allan Octavian Hume

career in the Indian Civil Service, Hume built up a truly vast collection of over 100,000 bird specimens from his own activities, from a wide network of contacts and from the purchase of other collections. At the time this was the largest bird skin collection in the world and was housed at considerable personal expense at his home at Rothney Castle, Simla, in today's state of Himachal Pradesh.

Referred to frequently as the 'Pope of Indian ornithology', Hume clearly saw the study of birds as something of a spiritual calling:

> There is no department of natural science the faithful study of which does not leave us with juster and loftier views of the greatness, goodness, and wisdom of the Creator, that does not leave us less selfish and less worldly, less spiritually choked up with those devil's thorns, the love of dissipation, wealth, power, and place, that does not, in a word, leave us wiser, better and more useful to our fellow-men.

Hume's achievements include the publication of at least two hundred papers on ornithology, including a number of monographs, the formal description of at least 148 new bird taxa and the founding and editing of the journal *Stray Feathers: A Journal of Ornithology for India and Dependencies* which appeared from 1872 to 1888. He is known today from a number of English bird names including Hume's Warbler and Hume's Wheatear.

Hume intended to produce a great work on the birds of India but in 1884, in his absence, his papers were stolen and sold as scrap paper by a servant. This event, coupled with the loss of one end of his museum to a landslip, caused him to abandon ornithology for good, and his collection was handed over to Richard Bowdler Sharpe and the British Museum.

Nevertheless Hume published some major works including *List of the Birds of India* (1879) and *The Nests and Eggs of Indian Birds* (1883). In the former he lists separately *Reguloides chloronotus* and *Reguloides proregulus* but in the latter he lists a single taxon only, now called '*Phylloscopus proregulus*' with the English name 'Pallas's Willow Warbler'. Hodgson's warbler from Nepal and Pallas's warbler from Siberia had now been formally linked.

In this latter work the widespread presence of the species in the Himalayas is made clear, as is the scale of Hume's network of correspondents. Many collectors were now encountering Pallas's Warbler, and an element of competition in finding its nest is obvious. Hume noted that 'Captain Cock has the honor of being the first to take, and, I believe, up to date the only oologist who has ever taken, the nest and eggs of Pallas's Willow-Warbler.'

Cock took several nests at Sonamarg, a hill station in Kashmir 'four marches up the valley of the Sind River' and provided the following additional details:

> The nest is of moss, wool and fibres, and profusely lined with feathers. Eggs, four or five, pure white, profusely spotted with red and a few spots of purple grey. Size, 0·53 by 0·43.... It breeds in May and June, making a partially domed nest, which is sometimes placed low down on the bough of a pine-tree, sometimes on a small sapling pine where the junction of the bough with the stem takes place, and at other times high up on the outer end of a bough.

The ornithologist William Brooks, another of Hume's correspondents, was also familiar with Pallas's Warbler, noting it in the valley of the Bhagirathi River, in today's state of Uttarakhand, where it was 'common in the alpine parts of the valley. It breeds about Derali [Dharali], Bairamghati [Bhairon-ghati], and Gangotri, in the large moss-grown deodars.'

Brooks published extensively in the *Journal of the Asiatic Society of Bengal* and *Stray Feathers*, and also in *The Ibis*. Over a dozen of these papers related to the leaf warblers and amongst this genus he described two new species - Tytler's Leaf Warbler and Brooks's Leaf Warbler. Clearly this was a group of birds close to his heart.

In 1872 he published in *The Ibis* a paper entitled 'On the breeding of *Reguloides superciliosus, Reguloides proregulus, Reguloides occipitalis* and *Phylloscopus tytleri.*' He was particularly interested in finding the nest of the second-listed of these species - Pallas's Warbler - and this paper provides a detailed account of his long but ultimately unsuccessful quest. Having learned through correspondence with Jerdon and others that the species could be encountered in Kashmir, he left for the region in April 1870. Arriving at the north face of the Ruttun Pir Mountain, south of Srinagar at an elevation of about 8,400 feet, he found his quarry to be plentiful: '*R. proregulus* was still in flocks. In the habit of congregating, and always being on the move from tree to tree, these birds resemble the Titmice, and are equally noisy.'

He met up in Srinagar with Cock, equally keen to discover the species' nest, and they set off together. After two days, however, Brooks turned back, heading for nearby Gulmerg, which he considered a more promising search area, but Cock carried on to Sonamarg where on his second day he found the nest he so desired. As Brooks noted subsequently:

> As far as I myself am concerned, I was completely foiled and never obtained a single nest. I looked only on the ground, expecting to find its nesting-habits similar to those of *Reguloides superciliosus*, whereas *Reguloides proregulus* builds in fir trees; and in this habit it appears to be allied to the true *Reguli*.

Pallas's Warbler was also noted further to the north-west, in Gilgit, then in the extreme north-western corner of Kashmir and now in northern Pakistan. Its presence there was reported to Hume by Colonel John Biddulph, a soldier and naturalist resident there as the British Agent from 1877 to 1881.

In 1873-74 Biddulph had taken part in the 'Second Yarkand Mission', an expedition across the Himalayas to Chinese Turkestan, during which he had collected avidly, acquiring most notably a new species of Ground Jay which, thanks to Hume, bears his name. Now resident in Gilgit, he made good use of his time to acquire further specimens and published his findings in a major paper on the birds of the region in *The Ibis* in 1881, with a further contribution in 1882. In the latter he notes of Pallas's Warbler: 'I obtained three specimens, two females and one male, in Gilgit in January.'

In 1898 J. Davidson published an account in *The Ibis* of a journey to Kashmir in 1896 in the footsteps of Cock and Brooks. Of Pallas's Warbler he notes:

> We shot our first specimens at Gangadgir on the 8th March, and noticed it later at Gund, high up on the hills, and also at Sonamurg [Sonamarg]. Nests, which we believe to have been of this bird, were found, one on a fir-tree, about thirty feet from the ground, and near the extremity of the branch, and two others on young firs seven or eight feet from the ground.

The species was also collected by the Czech palaeontologist and zoologist Ferdinand Stoliczka in today's Himachal Pradesh at Pangi, Chamba and, in winter, at Kotgarh, north-east of Simla.

By the end of the nineteenth century, the distribution and status of Pallas's Warbler in the Indian subcontinent were well understood. In 1889-98 Eugene Oates published the next great Indian handbook, *The Fauna of British India, including Ceylon and Burma*. It includes a detailed plumage description of the species and the following status summary:

Throughout the Himalayas from Hazara [now in northern Pakistan] and Kashmir to Bhutan. This Warbler also occurs, probably only as a winter visitor, in the Khasi and Naga Hills, in Manipur, and in the Salween district of Tenasserim [now in Myanmar], among the pine-forests. It occasionally descends to such low levels as the Dehra Doon.

Pallas's Warbler was now known to inhabit both the cool, dark taiga of Siberia and the lush forests of the Himalayan foothills. Between the two, however, lay a vast and, to Western ornithologists, largely unknown region - China. Here, as in India, the British would open the door to its scientific exploration.

BEHIND THE WALL

China had long been off limits to Western exploration but its isolation from the rest of the world finally came to an end in the nineteenth century. Trade with Western powers was initially restricted to the port of Canton (today's Guangzhou) through which the British purchased tea and silk. In return they began to sell opium, cultivated in India and then shipped to China. The business boomed and by 1820 there was a growing trade imbalance in favour of the British.

Alarmed by mounting economic losses and the increasing social damage of opium use, in 1839 the Chinese attempted to halt the trade by seizing a large consignment of the drug in Canton. Outraged, the British mounted an expeditionary force to blockade the port and, in the wake of the subsequent 'Opium War', Hong Kong was ceded in the 1842 Treaty of Nanking. Trading rights for foreigners were also established at Shanghai,

Ningpo (Ningbo), Foochow (Fuzhou) and Amoy (Xiamen). Many other such 'treaty ports' followed the 'Second Opium War' in 1856-60 and the signing of the Treaty of Tianjin.

It was in this coastal zone that Chinese ornithology progressed most rapidly, largely due to the efforts of a new influx of British merchants, naval officers, tea inspectors and customs officials. The key figure, however, was Robert Swinhoe of the British Consular Service.

Swinhoe joined the Service in 1854 and was stationed the following year at the then remote port of Amoy, about three hundred miles north-east of Hong Kong. From here he was able to travel the length of coastal China, including to Formosa (Taiwan), and soon amassed a large collection of bird specimens, eventually numbering some 3,700 skins of 650 species.

In 1858 Swinhoe circumnavigated Formosa and two years later was named as the first European consular representative to the island. He subsequently served as Consul at Amoy, Ningpo and Chefoo (Yantai) and also acted as a 'roving Consul', a duty which enabled him to travel to the island of Hainan and also up the Yangtze River to Chungking (Chongqing) in Sichuan Province. Swinhoe returned to England in 1862 with his collection of specimens, many of which were first described by John Gould in his 1863 *Birds of Asia*.

Swinhoe was the first ornithologist to explore this vast area and he discovered many new species, over ninety of which are still recognised. He is today remembered in a number of English names including Swinhoe's Petrel, Swinhoe's Snipe and Swinhoe's (now Rufous-tailed) Robin. His published output on the birds of China was remarkable, with a flood of papers appearing between 1860 and 1877, particularly in *The Ibis* and the *Proceedings of the Zoological Society of London*.

Writing in 1860 on 'the ornithology of Amoy', he distinguishes between the Siberian and Himalayan forms of Pallas's Warbler, noting that *Reguloides proregulus* 'winters here, and is of solitary habits' whilst *Reguloides chloronotus* is 'often seen during the winter here in pairs, going about from tree to tree in search of insects.'

In the early months of that year Swinhoe visited Hong Kong, Macao and Canton, also recounting his observations in *The Ibis*. Here he records *proregulus* as 'very abundant in the fir-trees about Hongkong during February and March', noting also that *chloronotus* 'resembled [the] above a good deal and at a distance were not distinguishable.' He was particularly impressed with Canton and its ornithological possibilities:

> Canton, with its fine old trees towering everywhere throughout the town, and its well-wooded surrounding country, literally swarms with birds, and I can safely assert that no place on this coast equals it for the number and variety of its Avifauna. If I had spent a few months there instead of a week or two, I could have swelled my collection into colossal proportions.

In the autumn of 1860 Swinhoe was attached as an interpreter to the British Army's march on Beijing, the culmination of the Second Opium War. However, as described in a subsequent contribution to *The Ibis*, his duties necessarily limited the opportunities for specimen hunting:

> ... the follower of an army suffers under great disadvantages. He is at all times interdicted from shooting within the precincts of the camp, and as soldiers always choose sylvan spots for their encampment, if the camp be a large one, he finds every grove monopolized by the army, and unless he travels miles away in a dangerous country, has little prospect of procuring much.

Plate 4. Robert Swinhoe

Nevertheless he found *proregulus* to be very common among the trees near Tungchow (Tongzhou) in September, with *chloronotus* also common in the same spot. He clearly enjoyed his time in the capital, noting that:

> We cannot allude to the parks of the Summer Palace, with their lakes and fine groves of timber, without making the soul of the naturalist long for a year's ramble at least in these lovely bird-frequented spots.

Amongst the most important of Swinhoe's publications was his ground-breaking 1863 'Catalogue of the birds of China', published in *Proceedings* (and revised in 1871), the first full checklist of the country's birds. This contains an account of *proregulus* in which it is described as:

> A summer visitant to North China, and a winter visitant to South China. Recognized at once from the foregoing [Yellow-browed Warbler] by its yellow rump-band. I have procured this, as well as the last, near Pekin [Beijing] in September; and I hence infer that this also ranges into the Amoor [Amur] territory.

Swinhoe's active professional and ornithological lives were not without incident, however. In another paper in *The Ibis* in 1866, this time from Formosa, he recounts that:

> I have been very unfortunate with regard to my scientific books. The two closing numbers of '*The Ibis*' for 1864 went down with the mail-steamer in a typhoon; and some other works have since been carried off by pirates...

Nevertheless, his observations continued. In an 1867 paper for *The Ibis* entitled 'Jottings on Birds from my Amoy Journal' he records his observations for 9th March:

We saw a male *Ruticilla ferrea*, and many of *Parus minor* [Japanese Tit], *Phylloscopus fuscatus* [Dusky Warbler] and *Reguloides proregulus*. The last we heard singing sweetly, and I thought, from its shaking song, that it was one of the Willow-Wrens, until my companion shot it.

Swinhoe also saw the species on Hainan in February 1868, noting in yet another paper in *The Ibis* that 'I saw a few in the gardens about the capital city in February.'

Others soon followed in Swinhoe's footsteps. Arriving in China in 1877, the English ornithologist Frederick Styan spent twenty-seven years working in the tea trade, acquiring a large bird skin collection and becoming an authority on the birds of the Lower Yangtze. Today he is remembered in the English name of Styan's Grasshopper Warbler, a close relative of Middendorff's Grasshopper Warbler.

In 1887 Styan published a short contribution to *The Ibis*, detailing a collection of birds from Foochow, assembled between 1883 and 1886 by the Irish ornithologist John La Touche. Here he lists 'eight specimens [of Pallas's Warbler], dated from November to March.' In his 'List of the Birds of The Lower Yangtse Basin', published in *The Ibis* in 1891, he notes of Pallas's Warbler:

> [It] begins to arrive early in March, and soon after its sweet and powerful song is heard throughout the day from the tops of the bamboos and firs.... Most of them pass on by the middle of April; in October they reappear, and I have observed one at Kiukiang [Jiujiang, a city on the south bank of the Yangtze in Jianxi Province] as late as December.

Styan was also able to assist the English naturalist John Kershaw in his 'List of the Birds of the Quangtung Coast, China', published in *The Ibis* in 1904. Here the Pallas's Warbler is described as common in winter around Hong Kong and Macao in the years 1901-03.

La Touche had entered the Customs Service in China in 1882 and remained in the country until 1921. During this period he made extensive observations and collections and, from 1887, contributed frequent papers to *The Ibis*.

One of these, an 1892 paper entitled 'On Birds Collected or Observed in the Vicinity of Foochow and Swatow [Shantou] in South-eastern China' records that Pallas's Warbler was 'very common from the end of October to the end of March. I have noticed it in full song just before its departure.'

Between 1895 and 1897 La Touche sent his native collector on four visits to the village of Kuatun (Guadun) in the Bohea (Wuyi) Mountains of north-west Fokhien (Fujian) Province. In the light of his success in the area, La Touche travelled there himself in 1898, staying in the village for fifty-one days and engaging local hunters to add to his own collecting efforts.

Here too he recorded Pallas's Warbler, noting in an 1899 paper in *The Ibis* that 'Kuatun skins are dated April, May and September. This and the preceding species [Yellow-browed Warbler] no doubt winter in north-west Fokhien.' The trip did not pass without a little adventure, however:

> While waiting in a sheltered corner for a threatening storm to pass, we had an unlucky dispute with some passing boatmen, who finally attacked us and would have boarded us if my wife had not, while we were trying to get rid of our assailants, brought a gun out of the cabin, which she pointed at them…

A further paper in 1906 on the birds of Chinkiang (Zhenjiang in Jiangsu Province) notes of the species:

> I shot a single specimen one year on November 24th, in a wood among the hills; and another year, on October 24th, I saw a number

flying about some gardens and copses on the plain. I have not noticed this species in spring.

Subsequently La Touche undertook a series of pioneering studies of migration on the Chinese coast, at Shaweishan Island opposite Shanghai in the Yangtze estuary, and at Chinwangtao (Qinhuangdao) on the Gulf of Bohai in what was then, prior to its dissolution in 1928, known as Chihli Province but which today lies in Hebei.

Observations at the latter site were documented in a 1914 paper in *The Ibis* in which the occurrence of Pallas's Warbler is recorded. In 1911 the species was observed between 14th April and 7th May, with 'many' on 20th April and 'a great many' on 7th May. In 1912 the passage period lasted from 7th to 30th April, with 'many' on this latter date. Finally, in 1913 it passed from 8th April to 17th May with 'many' on 16th May.

In 1920 La Touche published a further paper in *The Ibis* on the birds of North-east Chihli. Here he records Pallas's Warbler as a common migrant:

> It occurs from the first week in April to early in the latter half of May, and from about the 22nd of September to the end of October. Rushes of this little bird occur in early spring and in October, when they may be seen swarming everywhere and even occasionally penetrate into houses.

Finally, La Touche filled in the species' distribution in southern China in another paper in *The Ibis* on the birds of South-east Yunnan, published in 1923. Here he reports the species as 'common in late autumn and winter' and notes that it is 'found both in gardens and in woods'. He lists eight specimens collected in three locations between November 1920 and March 1921.

La Touche left China in 1921 and retired to Ireland where, between 1925 and 1934, he produced his great multi-volume *A Handbook of the Birds of Eastern China*.

Whilst the British (and Irish) were mostly active in the east, others were beginning to explore inland China and Central Asia, at the time an ornithological *terra incognita*. The key figure in uncovering the secrets of this vast hinterland was the Russian explorer and ornithologist Nikolai Przewalski. Following his first major expedition - to the Russian Far East with Benedykt Dybowski - Przewalski embarked on a remarkable career of exploration, undertaking four great journeys between 1870 and 1885 through the remotest parts of Mongolia, western China and northern Tibet, visiting such remote locations as the Gobi, Alashan and Taklimakan deserts, the Qaidam basin, the Lop Nor Depression, Koko Nor (Qinghai Lake) and the Altyn Tag, Tian Shan and Altai Mountains.

The fullest account is of his first expedition, contained in his 1876 *Mongolia, the Tangut Country and the Solitudes of Northern Tibet*. Here, in his 'Author's Preface', he acknowledges that 'the whole of Eastern High Asia, from the mountains of Siberia on the north to the Himalayas on the south, and from the Pamir to China Proper, is as little explored as Central Africa or the interior of New Holland.' Conditions in this high dry region were extreme:

> The baked soil of the desert smoked with heat, like a brick stove. Marching became very difficult; the head ached and swam, perspiration poured from the face and whole body, and a feeling of weakness and lassitude supervened.

Despite such difficulties Przewalski devoted much time to collecting specimens, amassing by the end of his fourth expedition some 5,000 bird skins of 430 species. These are now widely dispersed though many are in St. Petersburg. Amongst these are a few examples of Pallas's Warbler, Theodor Pleske's *Ornithographia Rossica* listing one from Kalgan (Zhangjiakou, north-west of Beijing and the gateway to Inner Mongolia), collected on the first (1870-73) expedition. Pleske also lists two from Gansu Province in July 1880 and one from the southern Gobi in September of the same year, all collected on the third (1879-80) journey. Przewalski contributed to the English ornithological literature, publishing papers in *The Ibis* on the birds of northern Tibet and on some new bird species from Central Asia, but he is perhaps best remembered today in the English names of Przewalski's Nuthatch and Przewalski's Redstart.

The other important figure in the ornithological history of inland China is the French botanist and naturalist Père Armand David. Ordained in 1862, David travelled to Beijing where he began to make natural history collections alongside his missionary duties. The plant specimens he sent back to the Muséum National d'Histoire Naturelle in Paris attracted much attention and he was subsequently commissioned by the Jardin des Plantes to undertake collecting expeditions throughout the country's interior.

Despite poor and declining health, he made three lengthy expeditions, the first (in 1866-67) north-west from Beijing into southern Mongolia. The second (in 1868-70) was his great journey into western China, travelling up the Yangtze to Chongqing, then to Chengdu in Sichuan Province and west into the mountainous Muping (Baoxing) District. Here he discovered such avian gems as Chinese Monal and Firethroat and confirmed the reported existence of the Giant Panda. On his third expedition he left Beijing in 1872 and headed south-west through Henan and

Shanxi Provinces to Xian then down the Han River to Hankou (Wuhan) and Kiukiang (Jiujiang).

On each of these expeditions, in addition to his botanical studies, he devoted much attention to birds, collecting and sending back to Paris a total of 1,300 skins of 470 species, of which about sixty-five were new to science, including two - Père David's Tit and Père David's Snowfinch - which bear his name.

He wrote accounts of each journey and several ornithological papers including a catalogue of the birds of China north of the Yangtze and notes on the birds of Shaanxi Province. In the account of his third journey, published in 1875 and entitled *Journal de mon troisième voyage d'exploration dans l'empire chinois*, he specifically notes the presence of Pallas's Warbler:

> 21 mars 1873. Pa-ko-chan. J'emploie toute ma journée a parcourir ces collines si proprettes, si jolies, dans tous les sens. Je capture une paire d'*Orites glaucogularis* et un *Reguloides proregulus*. [21st March 1873. Pa-ko-chan. My whole day is spent exploring these hillsides which are so agreeable and pleasant in every sense. I collect a pair of Silver-throated Tits and a Pallas's Warbler].

He clearly found the latter species a delight, noting it again two weeks later:

> 6 avril 1873. Ouang-kia-Ouan. Pluie Presque tout le jour.... Le joli petit *Reguloides proregulus* fait maintenant son voyage de migration vers les régions septentrionales. Du haut des saules et des rosiers fleuris qui entourent ma maison, if fait entendre d'agréables couplets, d'une voix assez variée et relativement forte. [6th April 1873. Ouang-kia-Ouan. Rain almost all day.... The pretty little Pallas's Warbler is migrating now to northern lands. From the top of the willows and the flowering roses which surround my house, it sings its pleasant, loud and varied song].

In 1877 he published with the French zoologist Emile Oustalet his major ornithological work, *Les Oiseaux de Chine*, the first systematic treatment of China's birds. Here he describes Pallas's Warbler, once again using the words 'joli petit' to describe it. Clearly he was attracted to the species:

> Ce joli petit oiseau... niche en grand nombre dans les bois qui couvrent les montagnes, et passe souvent l'hiver dans les provinces centrales et méridionales. [This pretty little bird... nests commonly in the woods which cover the hillsides, and often spends the winter in the central and southern provinces].

The full distribution and status of Pallas' Warbler were now becoming clear. Breeding in Siberia and the Himalayas, it was a winter visitor to southern China and an early spring and late autumn migrant through the country's eastern coastal regions. Was this the full extent of its range or did it occur anywhere else?

A EUROPEAN BIRD

In 1824 the young John Gould began business in London as a taxidermist. By 1827 he had become the first Curator at the newly-founded Zoological Society of London, a position which enabled him to examine any new specimen acquisitions.

In 1830 the new arrivals included a collection of birds from Nepal. Many of them were new, and Gould went on to publish their details in his 1830-32 *A Century of Birds from the Himalaya Mountains*, with a text by Nicholas Vigors and illustrations by his wife Elizabeth. In 1835 he assisted Charles Darwin with the classification of bird specimens from his visit to the Galapagos Islands.

Perhaps the most remarkable specimen to appear on Gould's bench, however, was not from Darwin but from the Austrian army officer and naturalist Baron Christoph Feldegg of Frankfort. It was a tiny Goldcrest-like bird said to have been collected by Feldegg in 1829 in Dalmatia (today's Croatia).

Gould had no idea what species it was but noted its bold supercilia and crown-stripe, double wing-bars and yellow rump. It promptly featured in Volume 2 of his 1832-37 *Birds of Europe*, in which he notes:

> A single specimen of this interesting little bird has been sent to us by the Baron Feldegg of Frankfort, to whom our acknowledgements are due, not only for this instance of his liberality in consigning to our care, at the risk of loss and injury, a bird probably unique in the collections of Europe, but for many other similar instances of disinterested generosity.

Unaware that this was the same species which Pallas had collected in Siberia some sixty years earlier, and believing it to be a member of the Goldcrest family, Gould promptly described it as '*Regulus modestus*', giving it the English name 'Dalmatian Regulus':

> We were informed at the same time that it was not known to any of the German ornithologists, and consequently that it had not received a specific title; this we have ventured to give, and suggest the term *modestus*, in allusion to its chaste plumage, and to the absence of the crest, which forms so conspicuous a feature in the other species of the genus, with which we have carefully compared it, and have no hesitation in assigning it a place amongst them as a distinct and genuine species.

Gould had found himself in the right place at the right time to document the first occurrence in Europe of Pallas's Warbler, albeit as yet unrecognised for what it was. Nevertheless, this was the first clue that this tiny warbler, still known only from the Ingoda River, might also occur far beyond Siberia. Further evidence for this would come quickly.

In 1837, the same year in which Gould's *Birds of Europe* was completed, the German marine painter Heinrich Gätke moved to the tiny British-owned island of Heligoland off Germany's north-west coast. Here he was captivated by what he described as 'that strange and mysterious phenomenon in the life of birds, their migratory journeys' which has 'for thousands of years called forth the astonishment and admiration of mankind.'

Heligoland, it quickly became clear, was an outstanding place for the study of bird migration, and Gätke was to remain here for some fifty years, collecting specimens and taking notes of the birds he encountered. He wrote up his observations in 1890 in *Die Vogelwarte Helgoland*, translated into English in 1895 as *Heligoland as an Ornithological Observatory*. In its Preface he notes that:

> My resolve to pass a number of years immediately by the sea, as a marine painter, led me to a spot which, from an ornithological point of view, is literally without a rival in the world. Here my artist's attachment for open nature could not fail to bring me in contact with the wonderful variety of bird-life in which this island abounds; and my desire to possess some of these creatures, so charming in all their acts and movements, led to the formation of a small collection. With the possession of these examples, however, there came a longing for a sound and fundamental knowledge of the material I had accumulated. Hence resulted many years of study of the bird-life of this island, and the comparison of its avifauna with that of other localities. From these studies and researches I was led to recognise that this little island presented an undreamt-of wealth of material valuable to Science, and indeed in this respect was superior to the proudest empire of the earth.

Gätke was not a trained scientist but he was an enthusiastic and astute observer, recording not just the birds but also discovering the patterns formed by their occurrences. He noted that most migration takes place at night and that much of it passes high overhead, only becoming visible from the ground when weather conditions are adverse:

> We have already laid stress on the fact that such portions of the migration phenomenon as become apparent during its periodical recurrences, are brought within the range of our observing faculties almost exclusively by meteorological conditions which are exercising a disturbing influence upon the normal progress of the migratory movement.

He understood that in autumn a drop in temperature and winds from the east or north-east could produce large arrivals of birds whereas mild winds from the west or south-west would produce very few. In spring, however, the most favourable winds for bird arrivals were warm light breezes from the south and south-east. He realised too that most passage occurs on a broad front, a view not shared by the contemporary ornithological establishment which believed in narrow 'flyways'.

Amongst Gätke's most notable discoveries was the occurrence in autumn of Siberian birds whose normal wintering grounds lie in south-east Asia. Though previously unsuspected, the appearance of some of these birds was, he discovered, both regular and predictable. The two most frequent were Yellow-browed Warbler and Richard's Pipit, both species whose breeding range lies beyond the Urals. Although barely recorded anywhere else in Europe at the time, Gätke noted at least eighty of the former, often two or three in a day, and many hundreds of the latter, sometimes as many as thirty, on one occasion fifty, in a day.

He also came across a number of other rarities hardly known in Europe but which were now recognised, through the reports of Benedykt Dybowski and others, to occur in the same area of Siberia. These included Dusky Warbler, Pallas's Grasshopper

Plate 5. Heinrich Gätke

Warbler, Isabelline Shrike and White's, Dusky and Red- and Black-throated Thrushes. Perhaps the most famous of his eastern rarities was an Eastern Crowned Warbler from the Lower Amur and Ussuri region which reached Heligoland on 4th October 1843. Despite the vast east-west distances involved - some four thousand miles - this was clearly an active migration vector.

Gätke employed the services of local people, most notably the islander Claus Aeuckens who was, in Gätke's words 'a devoted fowler and gunner from his earliest youth.' As a boy he hunted birds with round pebbles and 'At ebb tide he used to be much about at the base of the cliff, where, in the course of a walk, he would hit some twenty or thirty smaller birds, such as Stonechats, Pipits, Sandpipers, and others.'

On 6th October 1845 Aeuckens brought him a small warbler which he had hit as it flew along the face of the cliff. He had completely crushed it against the rock:

> Nevertheless, Aeuckens, who noticed that the bird was an unusual one, brought me one of its wings, which had remained undamaged, with a portion of the lower part of the back with part of the lemon yellow plumage still adhering to it. I had at that time no idea to what species this wing might belong, though I suspected it was one of the *Reguli*. Aeuckens, however, emphatically insisted that the bird was a Warbler. Accordingly I not only preserved the wing, but, as I am accustomed to do in doubtful cases, made an accurate drawing of it.

Progress in establishing its identity was slow, however:

> On obtaining a year afterwards, the first example of *Sylvia superciliosa* [Yellow-browed Warbler], I believed at first that I had solved the riddle; but on a closer examination, I found that, although the markings of the two were similar, their measurements did not agree. Several years later I read a short description of *Regulus modestus* (*Sylvia proregulus*), and also procured a skin of this species, but this also did not agree with my wing, as it happened to be an Indian specimen. It was not, however, until the

summer of 1879, when Eugen von Homeyer, on his visit to me, brought me, among other interesting objects, a Siberian skin collected by Dybowsky, and labelled *Reguloides proregulus*, that I was enabled to settle definitely that my wing belonged to the latter species.

Thirty-four years after its collection, new knowledge of the species from Asia and its increasing presence in European museums had unlocked the riddle. The identity of Aeuckens's warbler as '*Sylvia proregulus*' or 'Pallas's Willow Warbler' ('Goldhähnchen-Laubvogel' in the original German) was finally revealed and this tiny warbler could now take its place amongst the growing list of Siberian birds known to reach north-west Europe.

So lengthy was this process of detective work, however, that, in the meantime, Aeuckens had found another of the same species, this one the first to occur in Europe without being shot:

> On the 29th of October 1875, Aeuckens, accompanied by his nephew, Lorenz Dähn, again saw a bird of this species a few steps in front of him under the edge of the cliff. The bird was seeking shelter there against a violent east wind, and could not be induced to come to the Upper Plateau. Had it been shot at in the position in which it was found it would have fallen into the surf below and been lost. Thus our two shooters had the leisure, enforced in this instance, to contemplate the bright yellow plumage of the lower part of its back.

Intriguingly, Gätke also refers to a third bird though it is not mentioned in his main account of the species. In the introductory chapters, however, he notes on two separate occasions a '*Sylvia reguloides*' with its 'strikingly light-yellow rump' seen on 8th and 9th October 1879. This bird is referred to again within the species account for Little Bunting but now named *Sylvia proregulus* and credited to Aeuckens.

Gätke's observations attracted the attention of the British ornithologist John Cordeaux. He visited Heligoland in September 1874 and was astonished by what he found, noting that '... it may be almost said that birds of all countries are brought together on this lonely rock in the North Sea.' He wrote an account of his visit in a paper in *The Ibis* in 1875:

> On some nights the air seemed alive with the flutterings of thousands of wings and the innumerbale cries of birds. At early morning, after a stormy autumn night, flocks of winged travellers from distant lands are collected on the barren rock; for two thirds of the island is a mere bleak headland, exposed to every wind, and without the shelter of a tree or bush. Their number is often almost incredible.

Cordeaux lists many of the rarer species to have reached the island but makes no reference to the 1845 Pallas's Warbler, presumably because its identity had not yet been established.

Gätke also received a visit from the British steel manufacturer and ornithologist Henry Seebohm. After the first of his expeditions to the Russian Arctic (in 1875), Seebohm travelled to Heligoland the following year to see for himself some of its ornithological riches. He spent nearly a month on the island at the height of the autumn, writing of his experiences in an 1877 paper in *The Ibis*.

His paper recounts his exploits on the island and gives a summary of the most interesting birds recorded there. Here we find the first published reference to the occurrence of Pallas's Warbler, Seebohm noting that 'Mr Gätke's work.... will also contain irrefutable evidence that *Phylloscopus proregulus* (Pallas) and *Phylloscopus coronatus* (Temminck) [Eastern Crowned Warbler] have likewise been shot on the island.'

He takes the opportunity to quash any doubts surrounding the veracity of Gätke's discoveries. He admits that 'The list of

Heligoland birds is so varied that many ornithologists have doubted its accuracy' but assures his readers that:

> The authenticity of the Heligoland skins is beyond all question. During the time I spent on the island from 23rd September to 18th October I not only saw enough to convince the most sceptical of the *bona fides* of all concerned, but myself shot or saw in the flesh such a variety of birds, that I could almost agree with my friend Mr. Gaetke when he stated that he would willingly exchange his collections of rare birds shot in Heligoland for those which had passed over the island without being shot.

Seebohm also recounts his visit to Heligoland in his 1880 book *Siberia in Europe,* recording here that:

> Mr. Gätke... invited me to visit the island, to renew the acquaintance of the grey plover, the little stint, the bluethroat, the shore lark, the little bunting, and others of my Petchora friends, and to see something of the wonderful stream of migration which sets in every autumn from the Arctic region to the sunny South, and flows abundantly past the island.

Seebohm was impressed with both the number and variety of migrant birds, noting with enthusiasm that 'your next shot may be a corncrake, followed by a ring ousel or a Richard's pipit'. For days Heligoland experienced strong westerly winds, causing him to remark that 'sometimes for a week together you may diligently tramp the potatoes without finding a bird.' Eventually, though, the wind dropped and swung into the south-east and, as predicted by Gätke, a large arrival of birds took place, their collection including two Aquatic Warblers, a Little Bunting, four Richard's Pipits, a Great Grey Shrike and a Yellow-browed Warbler. 'Migration', observed Seebohm, 'is a question of wind and weather'.

Then, in 1892 (after the publication of Gätke's *Die Vogelwarte Helgoland* but before its translation into English), Seebohm published in *The Ibis* a full list of Heligoland's birds, the entry for Pallas's Warbler recording 'One killed in October 1845; a second seen in October 1875.'

The occurrence of the species was duly enshrined in the German literature in the third (1897) edition of Johann Naumann's *Naturgeschichte der Vögel Mitteleuropas*. It was also documented in the British literature in Henry Dresser's 1895-96 *Supplement to a History of the Birds of Europe*, the first volumes of which had appeared in 1871-81. This work contains a full account of everything known of the species' appearance, habits and distribution, drawn both from the available literature and from his own correspondence. It also includes the fullest description of the species yet published in English, based on a Dybowski specimen from Kultuk, Siberia held in the British Museum:

> Upper parts olive-green, the upper tail-coverts rather paler; rump bright yellow; crown darker than the back; forehead, a median line extending to the nape, and a tolerably broad superciliary stripe over each eye sulphur-yellow; lores and a broad line bordering the superciliary stripe dark brown; wings and tail dark brown, the feathers externally margined with yellowish green; the wings crossed by two distinct yellowish-white bars; underparts white, tinged with grey on the flanks, and very faintly with pale sulphur on the lower flanks and under tail-coverts: bill dark brown, the base of the lower mandible yellowish; legs greenish brown; soles yellowish green; iris dark brown. Total length about 3·5 inches, culmen 0·4, wing 2"1, tail 15, tarsus 0"67: first primary 07 shorter than the second, which is equal to or a trifle longer than the eighth; third and fifth equal; the fourth a trifle longer, this being the longest. The spring plumage is a trifle duller than the autumnal dress above described. In the summer the plumage becomes

abraded and paler, and the alar bands are less clearly defined. The winter dress does not differ from that worn in the autumn. The female does not differ from the male, except that it is somewhat smaller in size.

Perhaps the most intriguing part of Dresser's account, however, is his citing of Theodor Pleske's *Ornithographia Rossica* in which is reported the author's correspondence with Nikolai Zarudny, a Ukrainian explorer and zoologist resident until 1891 in Orenburg, about nine hundred miles south-east of Moscow. Zarudny's letters reveal the surprising occurrence of Pallas's Warblers around the city:

> In the autumn of 1887 I again obtained this species (I obtained one in each of the years 1879 and 1884) near Orenburg, under circumstances that would lead me to surmise that a migration had taken place. On the 3rd October a pair was observed in the Protopopen Grove, and on the 4th October a flock of about 15 individuals, with which were several Goldcrests; one was also observed in a flock of *Parus ater* [Coal Tit]. To judge from the characteristic call-note, this bird was observed earlier, between the 28th September and 4th October, in the woods on the other side of the Ural. In 1888 it again appeared near Orenburg, though in smaller numbers. On the 3rd October one was obtained in the woods on the other side of the Ural, and on the 23rd October again one out of a flock of five at the village of Neshenka.

These observations were of great significance, not least because Orenburg lies on the Ural River, Europe's eastern border. Also significant were the timings of Zarudny's observations, all in late September and October, and the fact that they involved multiple individuals. It was already known from Dybowski's reports that the species left its Siberian breeding grounds in September so Zarudny's birds were presumably on migration, yet their direction was not towards the wintering grounds in southern China but west, towards Europe. This prompted some obvious questions. If Pallas's Warblers were appearing regularly around Orenburg, and had already reached Dalmatia and Heligoland, where else might they be found? Could they actually be occurring regularly in Europe? And, if so, might one be capable of reaching Britain?

WHAT'S HIT IS HISTORY

The nineteenth century enthusiasm for natural history and specimen collecting was not confined to explorer naturalists in far-flung corners of the globe. In Victorian Britain it became a craze, serviced by a proliferation of new societies and journals, the most important being the Zoological Society of London, founded in 1826 (and publishing *The Zoologist* from 1843) and the British Ornithologists' Union, established in 1858 (and publishing *The Ibis* from 1859).

Few of these home-grown collectors, however, possessed any formal scientific training and fewer still were professional scientists but, with sufficient time and money, anyone could now found their own collection and acquire the status of an expert. Beetles and butterflies, ferns and flowers, mammals and birds were all pursued with enthusiasm and displayed with pride.

The study of nature was by now a socially respectable activity. With increasing prosperity and leisure time, the middle and upper classes sought healthy and morally uplifting pursuits. Providing both mental and physical stimulation, the study of natural history was ideal, and collectors, or 'gentlemen gunners' began to invade the countryside in ever greater numbers. Roaming the fields and woods, they could combine healthy exertions with educational self-improvement.

In reality, the quest for specimens occupied a distinctly blurred territory on the boundaries of science, country sports and commerce. Some rationalised their pursuit of birds as a scientific enterprise, a quest for valuable museum specimens and new knowledge. For most, however, the scientific motive was little more than a gloss. A much more powerful motivation was outdoor enjoyment. Competition was also part of the appeal as collectors vied with each other to build the largest collections or, better still, discover a new species. Inevitably, specimens acquired financial value and a whole economy of taxidermists and dealers grew up to make money from the collecting craze.

Meanwhile, improving transport and communications, particularly the development of the railway network, were creating new opportunities for travel. Those with sufficient money could now escape the cities and travel the length and breadth of Britain in search of specimens. Amongst the most popular destinations was north Norfolk and the village of Cley-next-the-Sea with, immediately to its west, Blakeney Point, a long dune-capped ridge of shingle extending westwards and outwards for four miles into the sea.

Two London doctors, Fred and George Power, were the first to come here in 1884. They had hoped for rare waders but, in their tramp through the *Suaeda* bushes and dunes of the Point, they had made an unexpected but much more significant discovery. On 12th September they encountered a veritable avalanche of birds including at least eighty, perhaps even a hundred, Bluethroats, a small Scandinavian chat barely recorded previously in Britain. Only days before they had found (and collected) Britain's third Barred Warbler, a large grey warbler from eastern Europe. The brothers wrote up their observations in 'Ornithological Notes at Cley and Blakeney, September 3rd to 19th 1884', published in the *Transactions* of the Norfolk and Norwich Naturalists' Society.

Following this revelation Cley saw a sudden influx of visitors keen to add to their collections not only a Bluethroat but perhaps even a bird new to the British List. Though collectors or 'bush-shooters' were already seeking migrant birds at a number of other locations - in east Yorkshire and north Lincolnshire, in east Norfolk around Great Yarmouth and the Broads, in east Suffolk and in Kent and Sussex - the discovery of Bluethroats on Blakeney Point propelled this previously unknown and unvisited shingle spit to a position of instant fame and celebrity.

The new visitors were to transform the economic fortunes of Cley and its neighbouring villages, bringing a welcome seasonal boom as the visitors required food and lodgings, the use of boats and the expertise of local gunners and taxidermists. At the centre of this new industry was Henry Pashley of Cley. In 1884, the year that the Power brothers discovered the Point's Bluethroats, Pashley became a full-time professional taxidermist and his workshop soon became an essential gathering place for collectors and dealers alike. Pashley died in 1925 but the same year saw the posthumous publication of his *Notes on the Birds of Cley*, a collection of bird observations from Cley and Blakeney Point in the years 1888 to 1924.

The most prominent of the visiting collectors was E. C. Arnold, a teacher at, and later headmaster of, Eastbourne College. His final book, *Memories of Cley*, published in 1947, provides perhaps the best and most complete account of the heyday of collecting in the area and includes his own bird notes spanning the years 1896 to 1928.

Arnold lists those who first collected birds here - the Connops (father and son), Reverend E. H. Ashworth and, of course, the Power brothers. Arnold's Cley contemporaries represented the next generation, amongst them Colonel W. A. Payn (reputedly the 'most scientific' of the collectors), T. E. Gunn of Norwich (famous for having downed an Aquatic Warbler and a Great Snipe with left and right barrels), Frank Richards (a London solicitor who never missed a season before the First War) and Clifford Borrer (who was to settle in Cley at the Old Manor House).

The collectors employed the services of a number of local men to act as beaters and to find, and sometimes shoot, the best birds for them. Richards would offer ten shillings a day and would also offer the same amount for any new bird which they were able to add to his collection. The Power brothers had hired William Brent, known locally as 'Old Bloke', but in Arnold's day the most sought-after for this work were Bob Pinchen and Ted Ramm (and their dogs 'Prince' and 'Duchess').

Whenever a wind from the east promised an arrival, the collectors would descend on the bushes full of anticipation. As a finder of rare birds, Arnold rated Ramm the most highly:

> He was a great authority on the weather as it affected bird migration, keeping a constant eye on the charts and always hoping for a 'through wind', and though good birds did sometimes turn up, when he didn't expect them, yet when he prophesied that they would be there the prudent made tracks for the bushes at once.

The techniques deployed were systematic and ruthless, Borrer reporting in a later article for *The Shooting Times & Country Magazine* that:

Every sort of device was tried to induce the birds to show themselves, including the dragging of chains and ropes through the bushes. But the only effective method was the use of a suitable dog.... what was needed was a close-ranging animal which would move from side to side in front of the guns, causing the birds to flutter forward above the shrubs or to fly out on the flanks affording the wing-gunners a clear shot.

Arnold participated in these activities with enthusiasm, his diary entry for 5th September 1902 noting that the bushes held:

one warbler, darker and greener, as I thought, than a Chiffchaff. It seemed to possess a charmed life, for I pursued it till my barrels were red hot and my No. 8 cartridges gave out. I was then reduced to shooting at it with a No. 4, after which it soared wildly up with hanging legs and finally dropped in thick bush, where I was never able to find it!

'What's hit is history, what's missed is mystery' seems to have been the prevailing philosophy, and stories abound of buckets of Robins and Redstarts discarded in the quest for rarer quarry.

The writings of Pashley and Arnold reveal a near-constant procession of rare and valuable birds. In 1890 there was a diminutive Red-breasted Flycatcher from eastern Europe and, in 1894, a Yellow-browed Warbler, amongst the first occurrences in Britain. Pashley notes of the latter:

The first Yellow-browed Warbler for Norfolk was taken on this date. This bird was shot with a 10-bore gun and very large shot. Its head was nearly severed and the rump and intestines almost entirely shot away so the sex could not be determined. The man who shot it fired off his battered old muzzle loader at the first bird he saw rather than take it home loaded.

On 31st October 1896 Ted Ramm claimed the greatest prize, at the time the rarest bird ever recorded at Cley. Henry Dresser's account of the occasion in *The Zoologist* reports that Ramm:

> found it amongst the long grass on the bank or sea-wall, not far from the sea at Cley, a locality which has produced many rare migrants, and at first took it for a Goldcrest, but on aproaching to within two or three yards, the bird being very tame, he thought he recognised a Yellow-browed Warbler, a species he had seen before, and therefore secured it.

A fuller account was later written by Borrer:

> It was the last day of October in the year of Grace 1896. The wind had been due east nearly all the month, and he [Ramm] and Bob with their two dogs were sheltering one afternoon from a furious squall of rain beneath the lee of an ancient railway carriage which formerly stood on Cley beach. Suddenly Ramm observed Duchess prick up her ears as a tiny feathered wanderer flitted past and sought the shelter of a nearby corner of the sea-bank. Bob remarked it was only a 'titty-wren' - the local name for a common gold-crest - but the super-intelligent Duchess followed the feathered waif out into the storm, and stood pointing at a great tuft of grass in which it had sought shelter. Ramm had seen just enough of the bird as it passed to recognise it as a warbler of some kind - certainly not a 'titty'. Duchess kept looking over her shoulder at him with such reproachful glances, that the gunner felt sure the bird was 'summat out of the ordinary' as he used to express it. Awaiting the next lull, he sallied out into the teeth of the gale and kicked the grass, where-upon out darted the little stranger, affording the easiest possible chance. When Ramm picked up the bird he saw at once it was something he had never encountered before, for it had a lemon-coloured rump.

Ramm's bird was of course a Pallas's Warbler, first identified as such by the Norfolk ornithologist Thomas Southwell who documented its occurrence the same year in the pages of *The Zoologist*. The specimen, which had by now been prepared by Pashley, was passed for confirmation to Dresser who on 1st December exhibited it as 'an adult female in very fresh plumage' at a meeting of the Zoological Society, confirming its status as a new British bird and one of the greatest discoveries of the collecting era.

Dresser also wrote an account of the bird's discovery in *Transactions*, in which he incorporated much of the background material on the species from his recently completed *Supplement to a History of the Birds of Europe*. The inclusion of Pallas's Warbler in Lord Lilford's 1897 *Coloured Figures of the Birds of the British Islands* represented its first legitimate appearance in a purely British avifauna but in 1899 it also featured in the second, updated edition of Howard Saunders' *An Illustrated Manual of British Birds*.

The occurence of Pallas's Warbler in Britain had in fact previously been published on the basis of a bird collected by the ornithologist and taxidermist John Hancock at Hartley, Northumberland on 26th September 1838. This bird had been identified by Hancock at the time as a 'Dalmatian Regulus' and its occurence published in William Yarrell's 1843 *A History of British Birds*. Hancock had noted that:

> Its manners, as far as I had an opportunity of examining them, were so like those of the Golden-crested Wren, that at first I mistook it for that species. It was continually in motion, flitting from place to place in search of insects on umbelliferous plants, and such other herbage as the bleak banks of the Northumberland coast affords; such a situation could not be at all suited to the habits of this species...

PALLAS'S WILLOW-WARBLER
Phylloscopus proregulus (Pallas)

Plate 6. Britain's first Pallas's Warbler (*John Keulemans*)

The record also featured in Rev. F. O. (Francis) Morris's 1851-57 *A History of British Birds*. It proved to be a false alarm, however. The specimen was reidentified by Robert Swinhoe in 1863 as Britain's first Yellow-browed Warbler, and Hancock corrected his initial identification in *The Ibis* in 1867. Ramm's Blakeney Point bird was therefore the first genuine Pallas's Warbler to be recorded in Britain.

Following its appearance before the members of the Zoological Society, Ramm's specimen was sold to the Norfolk collector Ernest Connop for forty pounds and passed into his collection at Rollesby Hall. This collection, containing almost 2,000 specimens, almost all from the Norfolk 'hotspots' of Hickling, Great Yarmouth and Cley, was then sold in either 1912 or 1913 to William Lysaght, a steel producer from Chepstow, and housed at the town's Castleford Museum. On Lysaght's death most of the specimens, including the Pallas's Warbler, were presented by his son to the Birmingham Museum and Art Gallery. The collection arrived in Birmingham in 1954 and remains there to this day.

WHAT'S IN A NAME?

Perhaps the greatest single influence on the development of Enlightenment zoology was the incorporation in 1758 of binomial nomenclature into the tenth edition of Carl Linnaeus's *Systema Naturae*. This provided a wholly new framework for the categorisation of the natural world. Previously there had been no discernible order to the study of natural history. Species had been named arbitrarily according to their physical characteristics and confusion had reigned.

In this new order, however, all living creatures were given a 'binomial', a two-part name in the internationally understood language of Latin or Latinised Greek. The first part of this name, always given an initial capital, denoted the genus, distinguishing a group of related species or an isolated, distinctive species. The second part was the adjectival specific name, never given an initial capital, which distinguished the species within the genus. Suddenly, order had replaced chaos.

Pallas's account in the *Zoographia Rosso-Asiatica* of his tiny warbler from the Ingoda River conformed to the emerging rules of zoological nomenclature. As well as publishing a full description of a 'type specimen' (the specimen from which a species is named), it proposed a Linnaean binomial. In this case Pallas assigned his warbler to the genus *Motacilla*, a broad category of small insectivorous birds within which he included a wide variety of warblers, flycatchers, chats and others. The specific name *proregulus* was a clear indication of the bird's resemblance to *Regulus*, the Goldcrest genus.

The *Zoographia* also gives us the name of the describer of the specific name (not necessarily the discoverer but in this case the same), the year of publication (as here, not necessarily the year of discovery) and the 'type locality' (the location where the specimen was first collected).

Pallas's Warbler was therefore introduced to science as '*Motacilla proregulus,* Pallas 1811, Ingoda River, Transbaikalia, Russia.' The date of publication of the *Zoographia* was a matter of contention for many years until, in 1954, it was fixed as 1811, drafts of the work being available at that time. Pallas's description and naming therefore have priority over any subsequent descriptions of the species in the years between 1811 and the full publication of the text in 1826.

Matters were not now fixed, however. Those who encountered the species subsequently had their own ideas about its affinities and how it should be placed within Linnaeus's grand framework. As a result, the species found itself allocated not to Pallas's original *Motacilla* but to other newly-proposed genera.

A particular area of uncertainty was whether Pallas's Warbler was more closely related to the Goldcrests or whether it was a true warbler, a dilemma reflected in John Gould's new 1837 name '*Regulus modestus*', a label which placed it firmly with the Goldcrests. This view was not, however, universally held. Alexander von Middendorff, by contrast, argued that, although it did indeed resemble the Goldcrests, its bill showed it to be a true warbler, and in 1853 he named it '*Sylvia (Phyllopneuste) proregulus*'.

In 1860 Robert Swinhoe referred to '*Reguloides proregulus*', the generic name clearly indicating the close relationship with the Goldcrests, and this name was also taken up by Wladislaw Taczanowski. Reporting in 1872 on Benedykt Dybowski's observations in Siberia, he notes the species' resemblance to the Goldcrests, remarking that 'in habits, mode of life, and nidification this bird shows affinity to our species of *Regulus*.' Taczanowski considered Pallas's Warbler to be unique, noting that '*Phyllopneuste superciliosus* [Yellow-browed Warbler], which has been placed by many ornithologists in the same genus with this species, is a true Willow Wren.' However, just three years later, Otto Finsch, then Curator at the Reichsmuseum of Natural History at Leiden, reasserted the link with the warblers, listing the species as '*Sylvia proregulus*'.

Hodgson's discovery of a new population of Pallas's Warbler in the Himalayas merely added to the confusion. In 1847 John and George Gray named his warbler '*Abrornis chloronotus*' (most sources cite 1846 as the year of publication but the date on which they were 'laid on the table' of the British Museum's Trustees - a preliminary to publication - was 9th January 1847). George Gray, however, subsequently listed it in his *The Genera of Birds* as '*Regulus chloronotus*', thereby perpetuating the debate over its relationship with the Goldcrests.

The Grays' proposal of a new specific name - *chloronotus* - also introduced the question as to whether the Siberian and Himalayan birds represented one taxon or two. Was Hodgson's warbler different from that collected by Pallas? The Grays recognised both *proregulus* and *chloronotus*, as did Edward Blyth who referred in 1849 to '*Reguloides chloronotus*' and in 1854 to '*Phylloscopus proregulus*' but in 1866 synonymised the two forms. Allan Hume did something similar, listing both taxa (under *Reguloides*) in 1860 and again in 1879 but in 1883 referring only to *proregulus* and allocating it to *Phylloscopus*, a treatment then followed by Eugene Oates in 1889.

The fact that this genus posed particular problems was recognised by Henry Seebohm in an 1877 paper in *The Ibis*. Here he notes that 'The *Phylloscopi*, or Willow-Warblers, are a group of about thirty species of birds, the synonymy of which has hitherto been in much confusion.' He continues:

> In order satisfactorily to determine the various species of this genus, an acquaintance with the birds in a state of nature seems more than ordinarily necessary; and this is probably the reason why this group has not been brought into better order by our cabinet ornithologists.

The debate over the position of the Himalayan population of Pallas's Warbler was still very much alive as the century neared its end. Heinrich Gätke noted differences between Siberian and Himalayan specimens, describing the latter as duller, and also identified differences in wing formula. He argued that the two populations should be treated as distinct species, proposing in 1889 in *The Ibis* yet another new name, '*Phylloscopus newtoni*', for the birds from the Himalayas. Henry Dresser, however, disagreed with Gätke's proposal:

> So far as I can judge from the specimens I have examined, the differences between the northern and southern forms are so slight, and the individual variations are so frequent, that I cannot support Mr. Gätke's views and do not, therefore, separate the species.

Plate 7. Henry Seebohm

Dresser treated Pallas's Warbler as comprising just one species but in the process was obliged to list no fewer than sixteen synonyms. Nor was this even an exhaustive list, as others were in use elsewhere.

Such taxonomic and nomenclatural chaos was the norm. Although Linnaeus had proposed some guidelines in his 1751 *Philosophica Botanica*, there were no generally accepted rules governing the formation, use and priority of names. Many authors embraced Linnaeus's binominal system but, as here, did so in an entirely undisciplined way, creating names according to their own preference or whim, whilst a few rejected binomialism entirely. As the number of new species continued to grow, authors independently described the same species under different names, unaware of, or perhaps without regard for, the work of others. By the second half of the nineteenth century, the resulting instability and confusion had become so great that it threatened the collapse of binominal nomenclature.

An early attempt to bring stability was the 'Strickland Code', developed by the British zoologist Hugh Strickland in 1842 on behalf of the British Association for the Advancement of Science (BAAS). Strickland's proposals, entitled 'Series of Propositions for rendering the Nomenclature of Zoology uniform and permanent' begin with the following words: 'All persons who are conversant with the present state of Zoology must be aware of the great detriment which the science sustains from the vagueness and uncertainty of its nomenclature.' His introduction continues:

> The world of science is no longer a monarchy, obedient to the ordinances, however just, of an Aristotle or a Linnaeus. She has now assumed the form of a republic, and although this revolution may have increased the vigour and zeal of her followers, yet it has destroyed much of her former order and regularity of government. The latter can only be restored by framing such laws as shall be based in reason and sanctioned by the approval of men of science.

Strickland's proposed Code went into great detail about how these matters might be resolved, addressing both historical confusions and how to conduct matters in future. The most important proposal was the 'law of priority' whereby 'the name originally given by the founder of a group or the describer of a species should be permanently retained, to the exclusion of all subsequent synonyms.' Generic names might change to reflect new knowledge of the relationships between taxa but, once proposed, a specific name should only be changed in the most specific and exceptional circumstances.

Strickland's proposals were adopted by the BAAS in 1846. They were, however, not universally accepted nor were they universally complied with. As the century neared its end, therefore, Pallas's Warbler (and many other species) remained hopelessly burdened with an ever-growing list of competing synonyms, its identity increasingly obscured by its own nomenclature.

Even British ornithology's leading figures - Dresser, Alfred Newton and Richard Bowdler Sharpe - perpetuated the problem, causing Seebohm to lament in the pages of *The Ibis* in 1879:

> ... unfortunately, during the last few years three ornithological works have put in an appearance, which threaten to undo much of the good which Strickland's efforts have accomplished. Ornithological nomenclature is once more disturbed by frivolous changes, and is rapidly drifting from the position of scientific accuracy to that of more popular indefiniteness.

The end of the century brought some much-needed clarity, however. A series of International Zoological Congresses was held, the first in Paris in 1889. A fifth Congress, in Berlin in 1901, adopted the tenth edition of Linnaeus's *Systema Naturae* as the starting point of modern nomenclature, established the International Commission on Zoological Nomenclature (ICZN) and proposed the 'Règles Internationales de la Nomenclature

Zoologique', a set of international rules which were published in 1905.

In Britain this progress was quickly reflected in the pages of *A Hand-List of British Birds*, published in 1912 by Ernst Hartert, Francis Jourdain, Norman Ticehurst and Harry Witherby. This was a remarkably clear and modern publication, very different from the confusing and often rambling nineteenth century literature. Its prime purpose was to list all the species recorded at least once in Britain but it also had another aim - to promote adherence to the new ICZN Rules, in particular the new rules on priority.

This agenda is set out clearly in the opening epigraph of the *Hand-List*: 'Nomenclature is only a means not an end, but without uniformity it is a confusion.' After the chaos of the eighteenth and nineteenth centuries, so evident in the case of Pallas's Warbler, this was the beginning of a new and welcome stability.

The *Hand-List* duly lists Pallas's Warbler as part of the British avifauna, notes the 1896 Blakeney Point record and summarises the species' known world range. Two aspects of this listing are of significance. Firstly, this represents the first appearance of the species' modern vernacular or English name but secondly, and more importantly, it introduces for the first time the concept of the subspecies and the use of trinomial nomenclature, in this case '*Phylloscopus proregulus proregulus*'. This treatment therefore distinguishes between Siberian birds, now assigned to the 'nominate' subspecies, and Himalayan birds, now regarded as of a separate subspecies, *Phylloscopus proregulus chloronotus*.

Trinomial nomenclature was a useful tool but it had endured a difficult birth. For a long time ornithologists had recognised that some species, particularly those with large continental ranges, could exhibit considerable geographical variation but rigid adherence to the binomial system had meant that similar forms were simply treated, often somewhat randomly, either as the same species or as a different species. Such had been the case with the Siberian and Himalayan populations of Pallas's Warbler.

Geographical variation was particularly obvious across the great expanses of the North American continent and it is perhaps no surprise that the idea of the subspecies was taken up there with the greatest enthusiasm. Its chief advocates were the army surgeon and naturalist Elliott Coues and the taxonomist Robert Ridgway. Coues took the first step in his 1872 *Key to North American Birds* in which he proposes the prefix 'var.' or 'variation' before each named form but it was Ridgway who took the final step to formal trinomial nomenclature in his 1881 *Nomenclature of North American Birds*.

At first, most ornithologists rejected the idea, refusing to use trinomials and continuing to give a binomial to every geographical variation. For example, in reviewing Thomas Jerdon's *Birds of India*, Blyth noted in *The Ibis* in 1866:

> I quite hold with Dr. Jerdon in his remarks on species and varieties, and think with him that 'it is more convenient in practice to give to each [recognized] race a distinct specific name, than to speak of them as Var. A or Var. B. of such a species', or, again, then to affix a double specific name.

This habit of recognising every variation as a full species had, by the end of the nineteenth century, pushed the global number of bird species described to almost 19,000.

In Europe the leading supporter of trinomial nomenclature was Seebohm. Having undertaken two pioneering expeditions to Arctic Russia - to the Pechora in 1875 and to the Yenisei in 1877

- Seebohm was more aware than most of the nature and extent of geographical variation in some species and he was a keen advocate of the ideas of Coues and Ridgway. Somewhat pointedly, he noted:

> Here again the confirmed habit of the older ornithologists of either treating these little differences as specific, or of ignoring them altogether, is much to be deplored.... I venture to suggest, as a punishment for their delinquencies, that they should be exiled to Siberia for a summer to learn to harmonise their system of nomenclature with the facts of nature.

He made little progress, however, in convincing a British audience of the merits of trinomialism although Hartert (Curator of Walter Rothschild's private museum at Tring) was a keen early supporter of the subspecies concept. Eventually it found more widespread favour, however, reducing by over half the number of recognised species, many taxa now recategorised as subspecies. The notion of the subspecies doubtless also appealed because of the opportunities it provided to describe and name new taxa and, as a result, enhance one's fame and prestige.

The acceptance of the subspecies concept in Britain was partly due to its endorsement by Harry Witherby. The journal *British Birds* embraced it from its very beginnings in 1907 and subsequently it was taken up by the BOU and *The Ibis*. Its place in British ornithology was finally cemented in the 1912 *Hand-List*.

Amongst many other matters, this resolved at a stroke the vacillations of the previous century over how to deal with the two populations of Pallas's Warbler. Now this tiny bird had both an apparently resolved taxonomic position and what would prove to be a stable scientific name.

Despite such clarity, however, there was no further sign of it on our shores. Surely it would not be long before another one was discovered?

THE HOUSE ON THE SHORE

The collecting craze continued into the early years of the twentieth century but its heyday was over. Public taste moved on and the cases of stuffed birds, once so popular, slowly went out of fashion. Its fate was also sealed by a change in public sensibilities and by the passing of protection legislation. A new idea had taken root - that wild birds should be watched rather than shot.

Ornithology progressed hesitantly in the first decades of the new century, however, and the rise in the number of active field observers was slow. The First War sapped the nation's energies and also removed a whole generation of future birdwatchers. Nevertheless, a new direction for British ornithology was taking shape.

The museum ornithologists had to adapt to changing times. Whereas the nineteenth century had been focused largely on classification and distribution - work which could often be done indoors - the development of effective and affordable prismatic binoculars brought about a revolution in how we studied birds. Now they could be identified and examined in the field as well as on the museum bench.

Though the move to field ornithology was resisted by some museum workers, its rise was unstoppable. It also heralded a new democratisation. Ornithology would no longer belong to a narrow scientific elite, its affairs managed by an educated clique of professional museum workers and handbook authors. It would become instead a mass activity, with the amateur playing a leading role.

The chief architect of this new philosophy was Harry Witherby. A champion of fieldwork and what he termed 'systematic observations', Witherby launched the journal *British Birds* in 1907 and within ten years it had incorporated the ornithological content of *The Zoologist*. This new publication ushered in a new kind of organised, purposeful birdwatching, Witherby himself noting that 'we are at the beginning of a new era in the study of birds in which the main emphasis will be on the *living* bird.' Soon new fields of enquiry began to open up, in particular behavioural studies and the study of migration.

John Cordeaux had been amongst the first to study bird migration, publishing as early as 1864 a paper in *The Zoologist* describing a great arrival of Goldcrests on the Lincolnshire coast in October 1863. Most inspiring to Cordeaux, however, was his visit to Heligoland in 1874 and his introduction to Heinrich Gätke and the concept of an 'ornithological observatory'.

Cordeaux began an enquiry into migration patterns on the east coast in the autumn of 1876, approaching lighthouse and lightship keepers for their observations, and the results were published in *The Zoologist* in 1877. A wider survey was undertaken in 1879 with the Scottish ornithologist John Harvie-Brown, with reporting forms issued to over a hundred lighthouses and lightships around Scotland and England's east coast. Their report was published in *The Zoologist* in 1880, leading to a series of even more extensive surveys, covering the entire British coastline, between 1880 and 1887.

Chief amongst the next generation of migration students was William Eagle Clarke, Keeper of the Natural History Department at the Royal Scottish Museum and a close friend of Cordeaux. Clarke visited the Eddystone lighthouse in the autumn of 1901 and the Kentish Knock lightship in 1903, recording many migrant birds including, at the latter, a Richard's Pipit. He later went on to explore a number of remote island outposts including Sule Skerry, the Flannan Isles, Ushant, St. Kilda and, most importantly, Fair Isle, between Orkney and Shetland. He was to visit this latter island many times, annually in the autumns of 1905 to 1909 and then in the springs of 1909 to 1911, by which time he was engaging the help of local observers to continue his work at other times of year. Fair Isle proved to be an outstanding migration site and, with much justification, he declared it to be 'the British Heligoland'.

This title was richly deserved for some of the rarer species recorded on Heligoland were found to be regular here also. The Yellow-browed Warbler was an annual visitor, with up to seven recorded in a day, and a number of Richard's Pipits were also seen. There were greater rarities too - a Blyth's Reed Warbler in the autumn of 1910 and, the following spring, a Thrush Nightingale. These exciting visitors, and many other of Clarke's discoveries, were documented in his *Studies in Bird Migration*, published in 1912.

Other Scots were also leading the way in migration studies. From 1907 to 1933 the so-called 'Good Ladies', Evelyn Baxter and Leonora Rintoul, pioneered the ornithological possibilities of the Isle of May, in the outer reaches of the Firth of Forth. Here they recorded many migrant birds and, as at Fair Isle, they also demonstrated the occurrence of eastern rarities.

It was the Germans who established the first permanent bird observatories - in 1901 at Rossitten and, in 1909, on Heligoland - but in 1927 Ronald Lockley took up residence on the Pembrokeshire island of Skokholm and added the study of migrant birds to that of the island's seabirds. A 'Heligoland trap' (a large wire mesh frame tapering to a small catching box) was built and Skokholm was recognised as Britain's first bird observatory in 1933, with the Isle of May established the following year.

The Second War intervened but its end ushered in a new era of enthusiasm for migration studies. The immediate post-war period was a fertile time for the new bird observatory movement and its fortunes went from strength to strength. New observatories were opened on Fair Isle and Lundy in 1947, at Spurn Point in 1948 and at Gibraltar Point and Cley in 1949. Others followed in the subsequent decade - Monks' House and Saltee in 1951, Dungeness in 1952, Bardsey in 1953 and Copeland and Portland in 1955. By 1957 at least fifteen observatories were in operation. All shared a set of common characteristics, notably a well-defined recording area comprising either an island or a headland with limited tree cover. Some had the added romantic allure of a lighthouse.

A Bird Observatories Committee was formed and a working definition of a bird observatory agreed. It was to be 'a field station cooperatively manned for the purpose of making continuous observations on migrant birds and for catching, examining and marking them.' In 1958 the British Trust for Ornithology appointed ex-Fair Isle Bird Observatory Director

Kenneth Williamson as its new Migration Research Officer and in 1959 it launched a new journal, *Bird Migration*, with Williamson as its first Editor. Standardised recording techniques such as daily logs and weather records were introduced and, for the first time, detailed analysis was undertaken of the movements of such species as Pied Flycatcher, Redstart and Whinchat. The bird observatory movement had now come of age.

The first attempts to interpret bird movements focused on the weather. Gätke and Henry Seebohm had understood its role in bringing birds to Heligoland but it took a long time before this relationship was more widely accepted, with most ornithologists continuing to believe in the existence of narrow migration routes. A notable advocate of this latter view was Eagle Clarke who persisted in his belief that Fair Isle was so blessed with migrant birds because of its position on a route from Britain through the Northern Isles to Scandinavia. There were some dissenting voices, notably Baxter and Rintoul, but they went largely unheeded.

It was not until after the Second War that such matters recieved a more thorough examination. Their chief investigator was Williamson. From his observations on Fair Isle he quickly determined that mobile weather systems, and more precisely the wind, were the key factors affecting the progress and direction of bird migration. In *Fair Isle and its Birds*, published in 1965, he noted simply that 'All our observations pointed to the strong probability that the major factor concerned was the wind.'

Accurate weather charts now enabled much more detailed analyses to be made and Williamson quickly developed his ideas. Chief amongst these was the concept of 'drift migration', a process by which migrants are displaced westwards across the North Sea to Britain. A small bird migrating at night, argued Williamson, flies in a 'preferred direction', correcting its course in relation to features in the landscape below. But over the largely featureless sea, and particularly in conditions of poor visibility, it will be drifted off this preferred course by the wind. The conditions which cause winds likely to drift birds across the North Sea are generally of two kinds, one 'anticyclonic', the other 'cyclonic'.

In the first of these, an autumn anticyclone centred to the north-east of Britain (typically over Scandinavia and western Russia) will bring cold conditions, clear skies and light northerly winds. These will trigger a departure of migrants to the south but, on entering the easterly winds on the southern side of the anticyclone, they will be drifted westwards out over the North Sea and will eventually make landfall in Britain. The second mechanism involves a depression in the southern North Sea which will displace migrant birds in the easterly winds around its northern flank. In this scenario, the associated frontal cloud and rain, as it moves along the coast, may bring larger numbers of birds to ground. Of course these two synoptic situations may occur simultaneously, each reinforcing the effect of the other.

These conditions regularly brought small birds from Scandinavia to the east coast observatories, in early autumn Pied Flycatchers, Redstarts and Willow Warblers with, later in the season, Robins, Goldcrests and the winter thrushes. They also brought rarer birds, including such exciting eastern species as Isabelline Shrike and Siberian Thrush to the Isle of May and, to Fair Isle, Citrine Wagtail and Thick-billed Warbler. Some of these were once in a lifetime birds but others, particularly Yellow-browed Warbler, proved to be of regular occurrence.

In his 1959 book, *The House on the Shore*, Eric Ennion tells the story of Monks' House bird observatory. Having worked for twenty years as a doctor in the Cambridgeshire Fens, Ennion had run Flatford Mill Field Study Centre in Suffolk before moving north. Here, on the Northumberland coast between Seahouses and Bamburgh, and opposite the Farne Islands, he found what he was looking for - a property right on the coast with the potential to become a bird observatory and field centre. Ennion describes his first impressions:

> Monks' House stands in the dunes in its own little bay.... Its sheltered position is more apparent when, walking along the beach, you come suddenly upon the clustered buildings than when, from inside them, you look outwards to a great arc of sky and sea and shore.... A burn, long known as Brock Burn, runs under the road and through the garden to fan out across the beach. Its little shallow delta of fresh water is a favourite meeting place for birds: eiders, curlews in the early mornings, smaller waders, gulls.

Here he developed a wide range of studies but, like all birdwatchers, he particularly valued the encounters with rarer species and the special affinity with place which they would engender:

> One gets to know the likely places; the sheltered bays, the best lookouts, the holes and corners where unusual birds have turned up on migration and may do so again. For ourselves and for those who have been here many times, the area teems with scenes of great occasions: the tiny cottage garden where, in a cabbage patch in the spring of 1953, we watched a cock white-spotted bluethroat - and the hedgerow where, in April 1957, on the second drive to a mist net, we found, and caught, another in all his glory - the quarry of the great grey shrikes; the gully of the grey phalarope; the sandy bay where the hoopoe was found digging for sandhoppers; even the little depression in the wall where a pair of roosting black redstarts were caught after dark in a butterfly-net. Such places and many more evoke hallowed memories.

Plate 8. Monks' House (*Julian Bell*)

Though not mentioned here, Ennion had already secured the great unclaimed prize in British ornithology. The second week of October 1951 had brought a spell of south-easterly winds and, at Monks' House, a large arrival of thrushes, Robins, Goldcrests and Bramblings. The full story of what happened next is recounted in the 'Notes' section of *British Birds*:

> On October 13th a willow-covered burn was being driven towards the garden Heligoland trap here, when what appeared to be one of several newly-arrived Goldcrests (*Regulus regulus*) flew into the trap. Goldcrests normally take no notice of the driving. I then saw that it was *not* a Goldcrest and, on going round to the gathering-box, found what I took to be a Yellow-browed Warbler (*Phylloscopus inornatus*). But, on handling, the prominent central crown-streak; the brilliant yellow superciliary stripes meeting at the nape; the sharply defined lemon-buff bar, a quarter of an inch

wide, across the rump; and the minute size decided in favour of Pallas's Warbler (*Phylloscopus proregulus*).

There, in Ennion's hand, was the first British Pallas's Warbler since 1896. This time, however, the bird was not shot on sight but was, in proper observatory fashion, described, measured, ringed and released unharmed, returning to the willows where it remained all day. The following day it was still present and in the afternoon it frequented the observatory's sycamore and an adjacent row of stunted firs where it was watched by a number of visitors from the local Natural History Society.

Ennion noted that 'There was great rejoicing when it was caught and ringed for it was only the second example recorded in Britain.' Celebration was certainly in order for, by 1951, Pallas's Warbler represented the most desired, yet seemingly the most unattainable, species on the British List. Fifty-five years after Ted Ramm's Blakeney Point bird there had been no further sign of the species. It had become a distant memory, a mere historical footnote.

Now, however, after more than five decades of absence, Pallas's Warbler was back, and foremost in the minds of many was an alluring thought. Might it be possible one day to glimpse this near-mythical bird?

OBJECT OF DESIRE

In 1955 H. G. (Horace) Alexander published in *British Birds* a paper entitled 'Field-notes on some Asian Leaf-Warblers.' Here he noted 'who would have dreamed that Pallas's Leaf Warbler (*Ph. proregulus*), the smallest of the genus, would twice reach the British Isles?' Yet only two years after these words were written, another of these tiny birds was found. This time it was again in Norfolk.

At the county's north-west corner lies the village of Holme-next-the-Sea with, to its seaward, an extensive area of grazing marsh, dunes and buckthorn bushes and, at their outer edge, a lone house in the lee of a plantation of pine trees. The building and its surroundings look as though they were designed to host a bird observatory, and it is little surprise that, following earlier ventures at Cley and Blakeney Point, one was established here in 1962.

The idea of siting an observatory here must have received considerable encouragement from the events of 17th November 1957. On this date a group from the Cambridge Bird Club had visited Holme. It was the nearest coastal migration site to Cambridge and a regular destination for the Club, indeed for a while it included this stretch of coast within its recording area. Their discovery is recorded in the pages of *British Birds*:

> On a field expedition of the Cambridge Bird Club on 17th November 1957, a small Passerine was flushed from an elder bush in the dunes at Gore Point, near Holme, Norfolk, by J. S. Clark. The bird resembled a Goldcrest (*Regulus regulus*) but was seen to have a yellow rump.... The bird was extremely active and spent most of its time low in the bushes, searching for insects. It sometimes hovered while feeding, like a Goldcrest, and the yellow rump was then very conspicuous. Occasionally it would make a short vertical flight from the bushes to snap up an insect, rather like a flycatcher (*Muscicapa* sp.). It seemed clear that it was a Pallas's Warbler (*Phylloscopus proregulus*).

This bird was initially watched at close range by five observers and was subsequently seen by the thirty Club members on the field trip. It was also trapped in a mist net, ringed, and photographed by J. L. Cutbill. Two of his images, appearing in *British Birds*, represent the first published photographs of a British Pallas's Warbler. It was also by some considerable margin the latest yet recorded in Britain. The Blakeney Point and Monks' House birds had both been in October, as had Gätke's birds on Heligoland, so this individual extended considerably the potential 'time slot' for the species.

Remarkably, 1958 saw the discovery of yet another Pallas's Warbler, this time even later in the autumn, on 23rd November, at

Plate 9. Pallas's Warbler, Norfolk, 1958 (*J. L. Cutbill*)

the ringing station at Sandwich Bay, Kent (a full observatory was established here in 1962). Again *British Birds* records the event:

> The 23rd was windless and cloudy with some mist, following a day of N. E. Winds at force 4. Other species present and not seen previously included a few Goldcrests (*Regulus regulus*) and Blue Tits (*Parus caeruleus*). When first seen, the bird was feeding in sea buckthorn and seemed to prefer this low cover, returning to it if driven out. Later, however, it was found in a rose-bed surrounded by tall conifers. It allowed close approach at times, but was somewhat difficult to follow with binoculars for it was extremely active.

A detailed field description follows as, unlike its predecessors, this bird was not trapped and ringed. It therefore became the first British Pallas's Warbler to be documented purely from field observations.

In 1959 *British Birds* carried an Editorial which announced that henceforth it would publish an Annual Report of all rare bird sightings. The publication of a record in this Report would depend on its veracity being accepted by a newly-constituted 'Rarity Records Committee' (later the 'British Birds Rarities Committee') which would assess and publish records from 1958 onwards. Until that point records had been accepted or dismissed purely at the discretion of the Editor.

The Sandwich Bay Pallas's Warbler was amongst the first rarities to be treated in this way and, following its acceptance by the new Committee, it was published once again in 1960 in its very first 'Report on Rare Birds in Britain and Ireland in 1958'. This annual 'rarity parade' was in effect a 'trophy cabinet' of glittering prizes, elevating each species to an object of desire and its fortunate finders to an avian 'hall of fame'.

The 1960s brought significant changes to British society and also to British birdwatching. Whilst the post-war period had been characterised by collective effort and shared goals, a philosophy best exemplified by the bird observatory movement, the new decade brought a new individualism. Birdwatching became a much more diverse activity, some continuing to enjoy migration studies and ringing whilst others branched out in new directions, seeking something less scientific and more recreational. In this context, rarities inevitably acquired a new and higher profile. Some preferred to hunt for their own, often pioneering new sites, whilst others attempted to increase their personal lists by seeing those found by someone else.

Perhaps the most desirable trophy of all was Pallas's Warbler though as yet few had managed to see one. Few observers were mobile and the dissemination of rare bird news was in its infancy. To see a rarity you had to either find it yourself or be lucky enough to be present in the right place at the right time. For the moment at least, relatively few people had either the information or the means to make travelling to see rare birds (what would become known as 'twitching') a realistic option.

In 1960 another Pallas's Warbler was found. *British Birds* takes up the story:

> On 16th October 1960, at Walton-on-the-Naze, Essex, we found a very small warbler which we first took to be a Yellow-browed Warbler (*Phylloscopus inornatus*), but which later proved to be a Pallas's Warbler (*Ph. proregulus*).... It was tremendously active, more so than any other bird we had seen. The whole time it was under observation it was moving and continually feeding with actions reminiscent of a Goldcrest but much more dynamic.

It could not be trapped, however, as it 'continually passed through the mesh' of a mist net. Then, six days later, came another:

> At 3.15 p.m. on 22nd October 1960, P.H.G.W. [Peter Wolstenholme] and J.M.B. [J. M. Butterworth] found a small *Phylloscopus* warbler in some buckthorn on the peninsula at Spurn, Yorkshire. It was no bigger than a Goldcrest (*Regulus regulus*) and from its small size, its greenish colour with primaries and tail slightly darker, its conspicuous yellow superciliary and centre crown-stripe, and its pale lemon-yellow rump, they concluded that it was a Pallas's Warbler (*Ph. proregulus*).

This bird was trapped, and the account in *British Birds* contains by far the fullest field description yet published of a British example of the species. It was also photographed in the hand. The bird was still present next day and was seen by many observers.

1961 was a blank year but 1962 brought another, now the seventh British record and the last to be granted a full account in the 'Notes' section of *British Birds*:

> At 14.00 hours on 12th October 1962, J.A. Bailey found a very small *Phylloscopus* warbler in some flower beds round a bowling green near the sea-front at Hartlepool, Co. Durham.... Its diminutive size and rapidly beating wings as it hovered to feed from an ivy-covered wall made one think of a humming-bird.

This bird was also trapped (but not ringed) and photographed in the hand. It remained until the following day, being seen by many observers until it 'disappeared down a Hartlepool street in the mid-afternoon.'

1963 was remarkable, bringing a record influx of six birds between late October and mid-November. Amongst them were the first south coast record (at St. Catherine's Point, Isle of Wight), the first to reach the south-west England (on St. Agnes, Isles of Scilly) and a second bird for Holme, Norfolk. This mini-invasion warranted a full paper in *British Birds* by Bob Scott in which it was described as 'quite extraordinary'. The paper briefly discussed the weather conditions at the time before giving a full account of what was being learned about the field identification of the species.

1964 saw another reach St. Agnes and the following autumn four more appeared, including another on St. Agnes. The 'Rarities Report' for 1965 noted that 'The appearance of this species on St. Agnes, a tiny island some 3,600 miles to the west of its nearest breeding place, for the third consecutive autumn is particularly noteworthy'. 1966 brought three more, including yet another to St. Agnes, and, for the first time, one was found in Scotland, appropriately on Fair Isle. Found at North Haven on 11th October, it was the earliest yet.

1967 was another blank year but the events of the following year were to prove historic. 1968 brought no fewer than eighteen birds, almost doubling the then all-time total. These included Ireland's first, and now the most westerly ever, on Cape Clear Island, Co. Cork, on 23rd October. The same autumn, described as 'astonishing' in the year's 'Rarities Report', also brought, for the first time, good numbers of Yellow-browed, Dusky and Radde's Warblers, all from eastern Siberia.

Noticeable by now was an increasing number of discoveries away from the traditional observatory locations. With more active birdwatchers exploring more coastal sites, the position of the observatories as the sole providers of rare birds was inevitably beginning to weaken. It was becoming increasingly obvious that rarities could be found in other places too.

Another tantalising 'in the hand' photograph - taken at Anderby, Lincolnshire - was published in the 'Rarities Report' for 1970. The same year brought the first inland record, at Weston-under-Lizard, Staffordshire, followed in 1971 by another inland bird in Norwich, Norfolk.

By the 1970s twitching was becoming more feasible and more popular. With an increasingly active, albeit informal, 'grapevine', the number of people travelling to see rare birds was growing. The early years of the new decade were disappointing, however. For those desperate to see this, the most desirable autumn rarity of all, had the trail gone cold? There was no need to worry. 1974 delivered a new influx, the 'Rarities Report' for that year noting that:

> There were some who feared that, after two years which could muster between them only a single record of this jewel of a bird, their eyes might never feast upon it. Yet suddenly thirteen came apparently from nowhere in the second half of the autumn and gave much happiness to scores of observers.

1975 was even better. This was to be a truly remarkable and long-remembered autumn for rare birds. At the centre of the action were the pine and birch woods of Holkham Meals in north Norfolk. Here, in a magical week in October, was found an astonishing parade of Siberian rarities including Radde's and Dusky Warblers, Olive-backed Pipit, Isabelline Shrike, Black-throated Thrush and, rarest of all, Britain's first Yellow-browed Bunting. Alongside these stars came record numbers of Pallas's Warblers, with at least 28 reaching Britain, of which three were at Holkham. The definitive statement on this famous autumn was penned by Ian Wallace, our most perceptive commentator on rare birds. In the Introduction to the subsequent 'Rarities Report' he notes that:

> October 1975 was the most magical month in the recorded history of rare birds in Britain. Even hallowed memories of October 1968 paled as an astonishing variety of birds appeared from Fair Isle round to Scilly, with the beautiful woods at Holkham in Norfolk providing the best ever mainland rarity watching.... One in two of the Asiatic vagrants was a Pallas's Warbler *Phylloscopus proregulus* and for every one there were at least four Yellow-browed Warblers *P. inornatus*. There can have been hardly a broad-leaved wood on the east coast that did not receive one of these sprites.

This is perhaps the first mention in print of a 'sprite', a designation which would become the widely adopted unofficial name of Pallas's Warbler, often appearing in a longer version - 'seven-striped sprite'. This was a clear measure of the awe and affection engendered in so many by this charismatic species. In the same Report the species comment for Pallas's Warbler echoes these sentiments:

Although no longer to be classed as one of the rarest vagrant passerines, this species is still perhaps one of the most attractive. The influx of about 28 in 1975 was the largest ever and it gained much by being set among a three-figure flood of Yellow-browed Warblers *P. inornatus*. For seven splendid weeks, the east coast woods were full of these two delightful, tiny warblers.

By the end of 1975 many observers had finally set eyes on their first Pallas's Warbler. Some still struggled though, Wallace remembering in his 1979 book, *Discover Birds*, how it:

> led me a most dreadful dance through the late 1960s and early 1970s. While most of my companions were seeing one, two and more, my luck ran solidly bad. In the end, I gave up chasing ghosts and decided that the little beast would have to come to me. Since 1974 it has, four times. God was in his heaven, after all!

After the excesses of 1975, 1976 was bound to be an anticlimax but that autumn's total of 16 was still the fourth largest arrival ever and brought the all-time British total to over a hundred. Numbers for the next three years were modest though another penetrated inland - to Blackmoorfoot Reservoir, West Yorkshire - in 1977.

Another milestone was reached with the first published photograph of a Pallas's Warbler in the field in Britain appearing in the February 1981 issue of *British Birds* - a montage of four tiny black-and-white yet mesmerising images taken in November 1980 at Sandwich Bay, Kent.

The total of 33 in 1981 was again extraordinary - and another new record - but this was utterly eclipsed by the events of 1982. This was a truly memorable autumn. In the second week of October there were huge 'falls' of common migrants on the east coast, including an astonishing 15,000 Goldcrests on the Isle of May on 11th, and, in what was another classic autumn for very rare birds, Pallas's Warblers still managed to dominate the headlines.

The final total of at least 127 was remarkable, more reminiscent of an irruption than the wandering of a few lost birds. The subsequent 'Rarities Report' noted that it 'could only be described as absolutely staggering; even in a year bedecked with superlatives, this flying fairy light has once again managed to steal the show.' There were some remarkable concentrations too, including no fewer than fourteen at Holkham where up to nine were counted in a single day.

Holkham had by now become the classic location for seeing a Pallas's Warbler in Britain. It is still perhaps the most reliable site in the country, partly of course because of its location but also because of its uncanny similarity to the species' breeding habitat. Its stands of pine and birch closely resemble the forests of eastern Siberia and it is no wonder that Pallas's Warblers seem to feel so at home here, often lingering for several days. They are, however, famously elusive, following the fast-moving tit flocks over considerable distances, revealing themselves in just an occasional glimpse of yellow stripes or the flash of a yellow rump. Their mercurial behaviour finds a ready echo in the nineteenth century reports of Benedykt Dybowski from southern Siberia and those of Nikolai Zarudny from the banks of the Ural River.

However, as well as blessing Holkham, the influx of 1982 also delivered birds unusually far to the north, with Shetland (including Fair Isle) logging 29 compared with a previous all-time total of just eight. Despite the large numbers though, not a single one reached Ireland.

There were only eight in 1983 and seven in 1984 but numbers grew again in subsequent years, with double figures each autumn and peaks of 61 in 1987 and 65 in 1988. Ireland did particularly well in 1985, receiving its second to fourth records.

Pallas's Warbler was now very much an expected part of the late autumn rarity scene and was being enjoyed by more and more birdwatchers. Away from Holkham, observers soon learned to search for them in stands of sycamore or sallow, the tree species most likely to host the prize.

Twitching was now a mass participation activity and the 1980s also saw the high point of Scilly's popularity as the essential October destination. Even those who lived away from the east coast could now easily travel to see a Pallas's Warbler or could hope to see one on their annual holiday on Scilly. Whereas news of rare birds had circulated informally through the grapevine in the 1970s, during the 1980s it was increasingly supplemented by information from the telephone in Nancy's Café in Cley and later from the 'Birdline' phone service.

Birdwatching, now usually termed 'birding', was also becoming more sophisticated. Better binoculars and the increased affordability and quality of prismatic telescopes helped with finding and getting better views of birds. In turn this revolutionised field identification. With plumage minutiae increasingly observable in the field, a 'new approach' began to compete with older more character or 'jizz'-based identifications. In a strange twist, some of the techniques once deployed in the museum could now be used in the field. The advances in knowledge were also fed by an increase in foreign travel and an ever more international outlook. Observers were now more familiar with the rarities which reached Britain (most of which were common somewhere else) and this new knowledge was in turn captured in a flood of new books and journals.

By 1990 Britain's army of skilled birdwatchers was finding so many Pallas's Warblers that the species was dropped from the

Rarities Committee's list, regarded no longer as a true rarity but simply as a scarce migrant, a marker of the year's turning. For many it has become an 'old friend', an expected but eagerly anticipated visitor to the 'local patch'.

A final farewell to the species as a national rarity came in Graham Catley's 1992 *British Birds* paper 'Identification pitfalls and assessment problems - Pallas's Warbler.' This began with an appreciation of its continuing desirability:

> Pallas's Warbler is, for most people, the epitome of a rare bird: a long-distance migrant, breeding no closer to Britain than 5,600 km away in central Siberia, only the size of a Goldcrest *Regulus regulus*, a mass of stripes of yellow and green, and hyperactive into the bargain.

In addition to the species' identification, this paper went on to discuss its dramatic upturn in fortunes and its occurrence pattern, noting that 'all the December records, four in number, have been since 1986, and future wintering, perhaps followed by spring records, is a distinct possibility.'

Throughout the 1990s and in the early years of the new century Pallas's Warblers have continued to arrive in numbers. New records were broken in 1994 with 161, and 1997 was even better with 171. By far the most remarkable year, however, was 2003 with a new record annual total of 313.

Since 1995 the species has featured in a new 'Scarce Migrant Report' in *British Birds*. The Report for 2003 noted:

> In 2003, this species enjoyed an outstanding autumn and a record year, accolades shared with Yellow-browed *Ph. inornatus* and Hume's Warblers *Ph. humei*. For four weeks in October and November, many birders found one or more of these three delightful warblers at favourite patches of migrant cover right the way down the east coast. What made the influx of Pallas's Leaf

Warblers all the more impressive was the sheer scale and impact of the arrival. The first, at Talmine Bay, Highland, on 11th October, gave no indication of what was about to follow. The deluge began on 13th when 14 appeared, followed by 33 on 14th, 25 on 15th, 19 on 16th, 20 on 17th and 18 on 18th.

The 197 recorded in 2004 seemed almost modest by comparison but was still the second largest arrival ever. The steep rise in the graph of occurrences is best illustrated by the annual means of the last five decades. In the 1960s this was just three, rising to nine in the 1970s, 39 in the 1980s, 83 in the 1990s and 90 in the first decade of the new century. Since 2004, however, numbers have declined from this peak but the species is still occurring frequently, and the all-time British total is now comfortably over 2,500. As predicted in 1992, there have also been records at other seasons, with several now noted in winter and spring.

Today the internet, pagers and mobile phones enable constant communication at home, at work and out in the field whilst digital photography produces images of previously unimagined quality which can be uploaded to social media and shared instantly. Rare birds, including Pallas's Warblers, are now within reach of everyone, if not in the field then at least on the computer.

This species has been with us through a remarkable transformation in British birdwatching but, despite its new prominence, the very mention of its presence still has the power to raise the pulse and quicken the step. For many, 'Siberia's sprite' remains amongst their favourite species, and the sight of one, or even the prospect of seeing one, brings a joyous rush. Even when far rarer birds are on offer, this tiny bird continues to grab the limelight, still one of our most popular and most wanted birds.

It is hard to define what constitutes a charismatic bird but the Pallas's Warbler surely encpasulates all the possible elements. Firstly there is an enduring scientific fascination in its arrivals. How does it get here? Why does it come? Where does it go after visiting our shores? Secondly, its numbers, although considerable, have not reached plague proportions, as have those of that other Asian invader, the Collared Dove. For most, it is still rare enough to trigger excitement and anticipation. Perhaps most important though, is its unrivalled aesthetic appeal. It is tiny and jewel-like, exquisite in its patterning and colour palette. It is truly an object of desire.

THE ART OF SEEING

Ornithology's legacy is mainly recorded in print, in the dry scientific text of museum catalogues, books and journals. However, the publication in 1830-32 of John Gould's *A Century of Birds from the Himalayas* represented the birth of a whole new genre - the lavishly illustrated handbook.

This was a small market, however. Production costs were high, print runs were short and the books were very expensive, affordable only by the wealthy. Nevertheless, over the next fifty years Gould was to produce more than thirty major works containing almost 3,000 illustrations, helping to foster a growing scientific and popular interest in the natural world.

The specimen of 'Dalmatian Regulus' received from Baron Feldegg was illustrated in his 1832-37 *Birds of Europe*. Although not yet recognised for what it was, this was the first published illustration of Pallas's Warbler. It shows two birds posed carefully to show both the upperside and underside and, as was

Plate 10. 'Dalmatian Regulus' (*J & E Gould*)

the convention, they are isolated on a blank white page, removed from any natural context and perched on a pale slender twig.

As with all contemporary illustrations, it was based on the careful examination of a specimen and intended as a detailed feather map. It was a beautiful and delicate image, thoughtfully composed and brightly coloured, but it was nevertheless a representation of a dead bird.

The image was labelled 'Drawn from Nature & on Stone by J & E Gould' but John Gould was certainly not the artist. In reality he was a poor draughtsman and to produce his great works he employed a team of illlustrators. For *Birds of Europe* he used his wife, Elizabeth, and Edward Lear, perhaps better known today for his nonsense poetry. Later he was to employ some of Europe's best artists including Henry Richter, William Hart, Joseph Smit and Joseph Wolf.

Gould is regarded by history as a manipulative glory-seeker, infamous for taking the credit for the work of others, including his wife, and ensuring that their proper acknowledgement was replaced by his own. His *modus operandi* was to produce an initial outline sketch which was then passed on to his chosen artist for the production of the final image, often using a new lithographic technique pioneered by Lear (and taught to Elizabeth) which involved drawing with wax or a crayon on fine-grained limestone. The layer of crayon deposited on the textured surface of the stone created the visual effect of graded tones. Following printing, the image was completed by hand-painting.

The artist responsible for the illustration of the 'Dalmatian Regulus' is not clear but it is almost certainly Elizabeth. Lear painted a minority of the plates for *Birds of Europe*, concentrating on the larger species, with Elizabeth producing most of the passerines.

Of the generation of artists to follow Gould by far the most well-known, and certainly the most prolific, was the Dutchman John Keulemans. Keulemans came to Britain in 1869 to work for

Richard Bowdler Sharpe at the British Museum and produced regular work for *The Ibis*, *Proceedings of the Zoological Society* and many important bird books including Henry Dresser's 1871-81 *History of the Birds of Europe* and Henry Seebohm's 1902 *Monograph of the Turdidae*. By 1911 Keulemans had published well over 4,000 illustrations, almost exclusively of birds.

So ubiquitous was Keulemans's output that his obituary in *British Birds* in 1912 noted: 'From 1870 to 1900 scarcely any ornithological work of importance was complete without "illustrations by Keulemans", and his sureness of design, combined with his facility of expression, made his beautiful figures always a delight to refer to.' Keulemans's work is characterised by its consistency, showing little change over the course of his career, and by its consummate rendering of fine detail. Scientific illustration required such accuracy but his illustrations are also vivid and attractive.

Keulemans illustrated Pallas's Warbler on at least three occasions, firstly (alongside a Plain Leaf Warbler) in Dresser's 1895-96 *Supplement to a History of the Birds of Europe*. This image was painted from a Benedykt Dybowski specimen from Kultuk, Siberia, as was his next rendering of the species in the third (1897) edition of Johann Naumann's *Naturgeschichte der Vögel Mitteleuropas*. This contains a painting of the species alongside some Siberian relatives - Yellow-browed and Dusky Warblers and a Siberian Chiffchaff.

Keulemans also painted around 150 plates for Lord Lilford's 1897 *Coloured Figures of the Birds of the British Islands*, amongst which was a third illustration of Pallas's Warbler, this time painted from the Blakeney Point specimen of 1896. The same image was also reproduced in Dresser's account of this bird in the *Transactions* of the Norfolk and Norwich Naturalists' Society. These images were all greatly superior to the pen-and-ink drawing of the species produced by George Lodge to accompany the second (1899) edition of Howard Saunders' *An Illustrated Manual of British Birds*.

Amongst the most prominent of Keulemans's contemporaries was the Danish artist Henrik Grönvold, one of the last natural history illustrators to publish hand-coloured lithographs. A skilled taxidermist as well as an artist, Grönvold worked in an unofficial capacity at the British Museum. Like Keulemans, his work appeared in the prominent scientific journals and he also illustrated a number of major works on the birds of Africa, South America and Australia. He is, however, perhaps best known for his warbler plates in Henry Howard's 1907-14 *The British Warblers*, one of which features Pallas's Warbler. Its full-page plate shows two birds exploring a tree stump, posed carefully to show the crown stripe on one and, on the other, the double wing-bars and the yellow rump. It exhibits to perfection Grönvold's trademark delicacy of detail and softly understated colours.

The early years of the twentieth century brought a new generation of bird artists, of which the most influential was the Scot Archibald Thorburn. Bird illustration from Gould to Grönvold had been essentially descriptive, a scientific as much as an artistic enterprise whose main purpose was to produce an accurate, albeit attractive, feather map based on a museum specimen.

Thorburn began the process of rewriting the rules of bird illustration. Most significantly, he was amongst the first to draw in the field, directly from life, thereby making the radical shift away from the traditional reliance on specimens. He was also amongst the first to consider birds in context, in their natural habitat, not just painted on a white background and perched on a conveniently-placed twig.

Thorburn's paintings are infused with a wholly new sense of being present in the scene, moving the representation of birds away from scientific illustration and giving it a whole new aesthetic and artistic purpose. This brand new approach is complemented by a peerless watercolour technique, his subjects appearing gleaming, polished and, above all, alive. Unlike the stiff and formal images of his contemporaries, Thorburn's birds look real and they were, understandably, hugely popular with sportsmen and nature lovers alike.

Nowhere is this transition to a new era shown more clearly than in the pages of Lord Lilford's *Coloured Figures of the Birds of the British Islands*. Ill health forced Keulemans to abandon his contribution to this work and Thorburn picked up where he left off, eventually producing 268 plates, more than half the total. The new Thorburn paintings made a dramatic impact and led to a sudden and marked increase in sales for the later volumes. He also contributed paintings to Dresser's *Supplement*.

Thorburn is rightly famous for his large watercolours of gamebirds and wildfowl produced for the sporting market but perhaps his best work is contained in the collection entitled *British Birds*, published in 1915-16. Here he painted Pallas's Warbler alongside a variety of other warblers including a Yellow-browed Warbler and, in another plate, again with a Yellow-browed Warbler, as the backdrop to a magnificent White's Thrush. Unlike the somewhat 'flat' renditions of the species by his predecessors, these birds were alive and breathing.

Thorburn represented a bridge between the hand-coloured lithography of the nineteenth century and the new twentieth century techniques of chromo-lithography and letterpress colour reproduction. Few had been able to afford the expensive nineteenth century folios but the new printing methods heralded a new era of mass production, bringing the work of Thorburn and his contemporaries to a much larger audience. His paintings were widely reproduced, most notably in T. A. Coward's popular 1920-25 *The Birds of the British Isles and their Eggs* and, after Thorburn's death in 1935, in S. Vere Benson's even more popular 1937 *The Observer's Book of Birds*.

The next published illustration of Pallas's Warbler was in Harry Witherby's *magnum opus* - *The Handbook of British Birds* - co-authored with Francis Jourdain, Norman Ticehurst and Bernard Tucker and published between 1938 and 1941. Produced just before and during the darkest days of the Second War, this was a landmark achievement. The plate of Pallas's Warbler in Volume 2 (painted, as was now traditional, alongside a Yellow-browed Warbler) was produced by the Dutch artist Marinus Koekkoek. Koekkoek was a museum artist, however, working from skins, and although his illustration is accurate, it lacks life. Rather than reflecting the new era of ornithological illustration, it represents a return to the pre-Thorburn artwork of the nineteenth century.

Eric Ennion's discovery of Britain's second ever Pallas's Warbler at Monks' House in October 1951 was a remarkable conjunction of a rare bird and an artist of rare talent. Although an inspiring teacher and a key figure in the development of the bird observatory movement, Ennion's greatest gift was as an artist, with new and exciting ideas about how to paint birds.

Though Thorburn had led the way in drawing from life, he had still been, at least in part, reliant on specimen material. Ennion dragged bird portraiture firmly away from its museum-based past, championing the discipline of acute observation in the field and drawing exclusively from life. He worked rapidly, aiming to capture a sense of immediacy with a minimum of line and detail, advising the would-be bird artist to 'train himself to observe and set down what he saw at once and quickly.'

Plumage minutiae and scientific accuracy were no longer important. What mattered to Ennion was capturing what the eye actually saw, no more and no less. He tried not to make detailed studies, but simply recorded birds doing whatever they happened to be doing at the time.

Ennion's birds were truly alive, not just a generic representation of his subject but an image of a particular bird at a particular moment. 'Birds are not hypotheses', he wrote, 'they are alive, very much alive, and not to be shorn of personality, not to be plucked from their surroundings.'

Like Thorburn, Ennion deployed an outstanding watercolour technique, producing loose, fluid, almost liquid, pictures in which the subjects seem to glide or float across the page. Unsurprisingly, *The House on the Shore* contains a montage of watercolours of his 1951 Pallas's Warbler (labelled 'a Siberian waif'), though sadly they are reproduced at a small scale and in black-and-white. Nevertheless, they convey both life and character. This is not a feather map; it is a living bird.

Ennion therefore completed the work which Thorburn had begun, transforming bird illustration into bird art and paving the way for later artists such as John Busby who shared his vision of drawing from life. Fittingly, Ennion was instrumental in the founding of the Society of Wildlife Artists in 1964 and served as its first Chairman.

However, whilst Ennion was taking bird illustration in a bold new direction, a wholly different approach was beginning to make its presence felt. The growing population of birdwatchers wanted illustrations to help them identify birds not in the museum but in the field.

This need had been answered first in North America where Roger Tory Peterson had pioneered a new diagrammatic representation of birds, simplifying their outlines and plumages so as to portray what was visible at normal birdwatching range. The nineteenth century illustrations, with the drab females often hidden behind their more glamorous male counterparts, had not been designed for field identification. Peterson's images, however, presented a variety of plumages according to sex, age and season. They were presented side-on and alongside other species for comparison and, to further assist the process of identification, key field characters were indicated with carefully placed pointers.

Peterson's first identification book - *A Field Guide to the Birds* - was published in 1934 and was an immediate success. It was followed in 1941 by *A Field Guide to Western Birds* and, inevitably, in 1954 by *A Field Guide to The Birds of Britain and Europe*, produced with Guy Mountfort and P. A. D. (Phil) Hollom. This first edition of the new European guide did not include vagrants but later editions brought the work up to date, and Pallas's Warbler was duly included in the 1974 third edition, illustrated in one of two new 'Miscellaneous rarities' plates alongside other much-desired Siberian birds such as Red-flanked Bluetail and Lanceolated and Pallas's Grasshopper Warblers.

Amongst the most gifted of Britain's post-war bird artists was Richard Richardson. Moving in 1949 to Cley, he quickly injected new life into Norfolk's ornithology, establishing Cley Bird Observatory and participating with enthusiasm in the heyday of the bird observatory movement.

Richardson soon gained a reputation not just for his remarkable field skills but also for his abilities as an artist. He rarely sketched in the field, however, and his work was done largely from memory. Nor did he produce great pictorial pieces but he knew the birds well and had a natural ability to capture their essence in a rapidly executed watercolour or pen-and-ink illustration. His paintings and drawings bridged the divide between bird illustration and bird art. They were useful for identification but they also brought the birds to life.

Richardson's knowledge of birds and his skill in representing on paper how they actually appeared in the field made him the ideal choice to illustrate Britain's first 'home-grown' field guide, the *Collins Pocket Guide to British Birds*, authored by Richard Fitter and published in 1952. In its Preface, Peter Scott noted: 'Clearly a new bird painter of great skill has entered the field.' Its colour plates, and particularly its black-and-white drawings, are still recognised as exceptional, but within two years the book was somewhat overshadowed by the appearance of the 'Peterson guide'.

The 'Collins guide' did not include vagrants, and Pallas's Warbler received the briefest of mentions in an appendix of rare birds. Nevertheless Richardson was to illustrate the species in a small pen-and-ink drawing in the Norfolk Bird & Mammal Report for 1963, the year which brought a then record six to Britain, including another to the newly established Holme Bird Observatory. With its masterful economy of line and delicacy of shading, it is an image of great charm and vitality.

From the 1970s, illustrations of Pallas's Warbler began to proliferate in an ever-growing number of new identification guides, both to British and European birds but also to the avifaunas of other regions. Initially, these were poor but many of today's leading bird artists have succeeded in capturing its allure, perhaps the most prominent being the Swedish painter Lars Jonsson.

Jonsson first came to the notice of most birdwatchers with a collection of five identification guides to European birds published between 1977 and 1980. The exterior of the books was unassuming but the artwork inside their covers was a revelation. Though formatted as a field guide, these paintings transcended the diagrammatic approach of Peterson and gave us birds which were scientifically accurate but which were also exquisitely rendered and instantly true to field experience.

The content of these five guides was later consolidated into a new field guide, the 1992 *Birds of Europe*, and additional species were added, including a Pallas's Warbler, illustrated in a brand new plate alongside Yellow-browed Warbler, Hume's Warbler, Firecrest and Goldcrest. Though conforming to the purpose and format of a field guide, Jonsson's Pallas's Warbler was a true 'sprite', poised to fly off the page.

MEANINGS AND MUSINGS

The meteoric rise of the Pallas's Warbler in Britain raises many questions. This is a species whose normal winter range lies in southern China and south-east Asia so what is it doing here? How does it get here? Why are numbers now increasing? Where does it go after visiting our shores?

These are some of the most-asked questions in British ornithology and they have for years provoked a proliferation of opinions, indeed there is scarcely a published discussion of migration and vagrancy without some reference to this species and its close relative, the Yellow-browed Warbler.

Bob Scott's paper in *British Birds*, seeking to understand the first significant Pallas's Warbler arrival in 1963, focused on the weather:

> The main feature of the weather maps from 24th/25th October 1963 was a massive anticyclonic system which engulfed eastern

England, much of Scandinavia and eastern and central Europe. The associated easterly winds to the south, in many places accompanied by cloudy skies, extended from well within Russia across southern Europe, France and south and south-east England.

Although, thanks to the work of Kenneth Williamson, the role of the weather in bringing Siberian birds across the North Sea was well understood, this represented only the final stage of their journey. The question still remained as to how and why they had flown to Europe from breeding grounds 4,000 miles away. The answer, as alluded to by Scott, lay further east, in Russia.

Heinrich Gätke had been quick to realise the importance of the weather in the arrival of Siberian birds, noting that they only appeared in years which saw easterly or south-easterly winds at the right time, and his correspondence with meteorologists in Russia confirmed that those years which saw the greatest influxes were those in which the easterly airflow extended most deeply into Siberia. On such occasions, multiple arrivals of a range of eastern species were to be expected.

However, the wind could not be the only factor at work. Over a featureless area such as the North Sea a bird would be vulnerable to wind displacement but when flying over land it could stop at any point it wished. These birds were not therefore just 'drift migrants', blown across the whole width of Russia by the wind. Some other mechanism must be involved.

To address this question Williamson drew a distinction between European migrants and Siberian wanderers. The former were drifted across the North Sea in the course of their normal migration but the Siberian birds were, he argued, on what he termed 'post-juvenile dispersal', not a true purposeful migration towards the wintering grounds but a random initial movement away from the breeding area. However, whilst the wind was not the prime cause of these movements, it nevertheless had a role in facilitating and extending them.

Following the sudden and dramatic increase in the number of Siberian birds (now including Pallas's Warblers) reaching Britain in the autumns of 1968, 1974 and 1975, Kevin Baker published a paper in *Bird Study* in which he provided further evidence in support of Williamson's notion of post-juvenile dispersal directed by the weather. Baker noted that in early October in each of these three autumns a large anticyclone had become established over Siberia, producing a steady and long-range easterly airflow along its southern flank. This was, he argued, responsible for the particular prominence of Siberian birds in Britain in these autumns. By contrast, in autumns with fewer Siberian birds, these anticyclones were too small to have any effect, were located in the 'wrong' place or did not persist.

A similar paper by D. H. Howey and M. Bell, published in *British Birds* in 1985, analysed the even more dramatic arrival of Pallas's Warblers in October 1982. In that year a Siberian anticyclone had developed particularly early, enabling the birds to reach Europe from late September. Later birds had, they argued, arrived in the easterly winds around the top of a low pressure area moving north-east from the Caspian Sea, reaching Scandinavia and the Baltic region. Here they became caught up in the 'fall' conditions around the North Sea in the second week of October.

This mechanism - wind-assisted dispersal - was supported by the meteorologist Norman Elkins in his 1983 book *Weather and Bird Behaviour* and was also invoked in his 1991 paper in *British Birds* discussing the arrival of Siberian passerines in Britain in autumn 1988. Here he noted the development that autumn of 'an intense anticyclone which extended much farther west into Europe than normal, and which created a strong mean easterly airflow on its southern flank as far west as the Black Sea.'

In 1987 Baker and Graham Catley published an analysis of the 1985 influx of Yellow-browed Warblers, which also brought with it some Pallas's Warblers. They agreed with previous authors that these events could be explained at least in part by the weather patterns over Russia, in particular the development and persistence of large anticyclones.

However, not all authors supported the 'random dispersal and downwind displacement' model. As early as 1966 K. B. Rooke had proposed an alternative concept built entirely around the Pallas's Warbler. This notion, termed 'reversed migration', assumed that some birds have a genetic mutation or defect in their internal compass which makes them fly in precisely the opposite direction to that required to reach the wintering areas, reaching western Europe on a great circle track.

These ideas were taken up in 1969 by Jørgen Rabøl in a *British Birds* paper entitled 'Reversed migration as the cause of westward vagrancy by four *Phylloscopus* warblers.' He noted that many Siberian birds had an initial eastward heading on their autumn migration before they turned south to the wintering area, thereby avoiding the great inhospitable heart of Asia - the Gobi Desert, the Tibetan Plateau and the Himalayas. If something went wrong with the navigational capacity of some of these birds, resulting in their flying in exactly the opposite direction to this initial eastward trajectory, they would find themselves on a westerly track towards Europe.

Rabøl also noted that a strict east-west trajectory could be inferred from the distribution of Siberian birds in Britain, the more northerly-breeding Yellow-browed Warbler occurring in larger numbers further north, particularly in Shetland, with the

Plate 11. Pallas's Warbler, Norfolk, 2010 (*Penny Clarke*)

more southerly-breeding Pallas's Warbler appearing further south, in eastern and southern England. The breeding distribution was therefore reflected in the pattern of occurrence in Britain and indicated that reversed migration was stable over great distances. Rabøl kept an open mind on the subject, however:

> This hypothesis of reversed migration and my treatment of the material are open to criticism, and the role which weather factors play in channelling randomly dispersed birds in the same direction should not be underestimated. I think, however, that the phenomenon of reversed migration contributes significantly to the autumn occurrences of east European and Asiatic passerines in western Europe.

In 1997 David Cottridge and Keith Vinicombe extended this idea in *Rare Birds in Britain & Ireland: A Photographic Record*. They proposed the existence of a 'vagrancy shadow', an area corresponding to a mirror image of the normal route to winter quarters. For example, the vagrancy shadow of Pallas's Warbler falls across north-west Europe, explaining its appearance there, whilst that of, for example, Collared Flycatcher (breeding in eastern Europe and wintering in East Africa) does not, explaining that species' near-absence in Britain in autumn. The vagrancy shadow was intended to explain existing occurrence patterns but it could also, they argued, predict the likelihood of occurrence of other species too.

In a 1998 paper in *Ringing and Migration* Kasper Thorup added to the debate. Having trapped a number of both Pallas's and Yellow-browed Warblers in Denmark in autumn 1994, he determined through a series of orientation cage experiments that the birds were intent on an onward journey between west and south-west. This corresponded with them taking a great circle route west from Siberia then south-west through Europe.

In a further paper in 2004 he argued once more that 'pure wind drift does not offer any satisfactory explanation for the occurrence of reverse migrants, and the explanation is more likely to be linked to the orientation system.' He also suggested that species with a more easterly migration track (such as Pallas's Warbler) may have more trouble separating east from west than those species with a more southerly migration. The reversed migration of Siberian passerines to Europe may therefore arise from an inability to tell east from west.

These competing theories have been hotly debated, and each clearly has some degree of accordance with what is observed. There are, however, particular problems with the reversed migration theory. Thomas Alerstam discussed these in 1990 in his book, *Bird Migration*. Here he postulated that the apparent westward track of Pallas's Warblers on a 180 degree reversed course was an illusion. Birds disperse in all directions, he argued, but only those passing through hospitable regions survive to be recorded. Thus any Pallas's Warblers flying east into the Pacific, north to the Arctic Ocean, or south-west into the mountains and deserts of Central Asia probably do not survive whereas those on a westerly heading find food throughout the temperate forest zone all the way to Europe.

Other factors are at work too. Not only will westbound birds have the highest survival rate but they will reach north-west Europe, an area with a high density of birdwatchers, many of whom will be actively looking for Pallas's Warblers. The double effect of a high survival rate and a high rate of detection produces the illusion of a narrow migratory path.

Further evidence of a wide scatter of birds comes from the fact that, despite a much lower density of birdwatchers, Pallas's Warblers nevertheless *are* found in directions other than due west. In autumn the species has wandered far to the east, regularly reaching Japan. It even reached St. Lawrence Island, Alaska on 25th-26th September 2006. There is a wide scatter of records in southern Europe too and it has also occurred in Israel and Iran.

Alerstam went on to argue that the differing distribution in Britain of Pallas's and Yellow-browed Warblers did not indicate a precisely directed reversed migration either, being merely a consequence of their arrival dates. Yellow-browed Warblers arrive earlier in the autumn, while a northern route with sufficient food to sustain a migrant is still open, whilst the later-arriving Pallas's Warblers only have more southerly routes available. Furthermore, the precise location of arrivals is largely dictated by local weather conditions over the North Sea. He concluded: 'I therefore consider that there are hardly any convincing basic facts that support the theory of a particular reversed migration.'

In 2000 a paper by John Phillips in *Ringing and Migration* poured further cold water on the reversed migration theory. Most problematically, the theory relied on the notion of a defective bird, one with a genetic abnormality. Such a condition should by definition be uncommon. However, the tendency to migrate in the wrong direction involved not just a few individuals but large numbers of birds. Although a few might genuinely be defective, it seemed improbable that this condition would affect such a large proportion of the population.

There was also the question of the dramatic increase in the numbers of Pallas's Warblers reaching Britain since the 1960s which, even allowing for the greatly increased number of observers, appeared to be genuine. Any genetic mutation should, in theory, be subject to natural selection. In other words, differential survival should progressively eliminate those birds taking a radically wrong direction. This was evidently not the case, however, as not only were Pallas's Warblers continuing to come to Europe but their numbers were increasing. Some other factor or factors must be involved.

To explain this conundrum Phillips proposed a novel idea. Was it possible, he asked, that some Siberian vagrants to Europe were surviving the winter and returning to Siberia to breed, passing on their genes for wrong orientations? Might this be the answer to the other burning question as to where these birds went after passing through north-west Europe?

The debate was revisited in 2003 by James Gilroy and Alex Lees in a paper in *British Birds*. These authors reprised the idea that the birds occurring in Europe were not true vagrants at all but regular migrants (which they termed 'pseudo-vagrants') on their way to newly established but as yet undiscovered wintering areas, probably in south-west Europe and north-west Africa. In this scenario, the rising numbers were a reflection of high winter survival rates which had led to a progressive increase of the 'west-orientating' genotypes in the Siberian breeding population. Though recognising that there was so far little direct evidence to support this contention, the authors argued that a wide but thin distribution of wintering birds over extensive areas largely devoid of birdwatchers would make their detection difficult.

The lack of records in spring was unsurprising given the relatively small numbers of birds, the traditionally rapid nature of spring migration and the fact that a different route was probably involved. In other words, any spring migrants would be unlikely to pass through the areas where they occurred in autumn and would therefore be barely detectable.

These ideas were subsequently challenged by Eduardo de Juana in a 2008 paper in *Ardeola*. De Juana noted that, contrary to the theory that Pallas's Warblers were migrating to, and perhaps even wintering in, the Iberian Peninsula, there were actually very few records, particularly in north-west Spain, the region most likely to receive them. The few which did reach Spain were instead concentrated in the east of the country. He argued that the number and distribution of records in Spain was real, not due to observer factors, and that just a small fraction of the birds visiting Scandinavia and Britain move south-west through the Iberian Peninsula. Taking all this into account, he put forward a new hypothesis: that once birds reach north-west Europe they redirect their migration to the south-east.

The recent dramatic increase in the numbers of Pallas's Warblers reaching Europe and speculation about new wintering areas changes the nature of the debate from one about vagrancy to one about population dynamics. It has been well established that vagrants can be 'pioneers', representing the expanding fringe of a growing population, but in the case of the Pallas's Warbler there is no published evidence either of a population increase or of a range expansion.

Could the Pallas's Warbler instead be doing what the Blackcap has already done? British-breeding Blackcaps migrate south in winter but some from Central Europe have adopted a new north-westward migration in autumn to winter in the relatively mild conditions found in Britain. This strategy has proved successful, and more European Blackcaps are now wintering here. This shows that genetically-controlled migratory behaviour is not fixed. Indeed it can be surprisingly flexible, with new migration habits, routes and wintering areas adopted within just a few generations. This flexibility may be a significant asset. In an era of changing climate and increasing human modification of the landscape, might species able to adapt in this way and rapidly evolve new and flexible strategies greatly enhance their survival prospects?

There are still few concrete answers to any of the problems presented here. For the moment, therefore, the Pallas's Warbler continues to confound, posing some of the most topical and intractable questions in ornithology.

SPLIT DECISIONS

The publication of the 1912 *A Hand-List of British Birds* marked the beginning of a period of relative taxonomic stability, at least at species level. For much of the twentieth century the attention of taxonomists was focused on documenting geographical variation and exploring the limits of the subspecies concept.

In 1920 a new subspecies of Pallas's Warbler, '*simlaensis*', was described by Claud Ticehurst (younger brother of Norman Ticehurst) from a specimen collected in Simla, India in 1880, firstly forming part of the Hume Collection and now at the British Museum. A further subspecies, '*forresti*' (named for the botanist George Forrest), was described in 1921 by Walter Rothschild from a specimen collected in 1918 in the Lijiang Range in China's Yunnan Province. It too is now at the British Museum. Then, in 1922 John La Touche described a fifth subspecies, '*yunnanensis*', from Mengtsz (Mengzi) in Yunnan, proposing it three years later as a distinct species. Finally, in

1933 the German ornithologist Wilhelm Meise described the subspecies '*kansuensis*' from a specimen from Lauhukou, near Xining. Until 1928 this locality was in China's Gansu Province but thereafter fell in Qinghai Province.

This represented the 'high water mark' of trinomialism, with the rest of the century seeing a slow process of resistance and retrenchment. In 1938 Claud Ticehurst published *A Systematic Review of the Genus Phylloscopus*. This recognised nominate *proregulus*, *chloronotus*, *simlaensis* and *forresti*. It also accepted *kansuensis* but regarded it as very poorly differentiated, 'an intergradational form' between nominate *proregulus* and *chloronotus*. The subspecies *yunnanensis* was, however, regarded as invalid, a synonym of *chloronotus*.

The 1938-41 'Witherby Handbook' recognised the existence of 'allied races in Himalayas, China (Szechwan, Yunnan, and Kansu).' These are defined as '*chloronotus* (Nepal), *simlaensis* (Gilgit, Kashmir) and *forresti* (Yunnan).' With the exception of the omission of *kansuensis*, the synergy with Ticehurst's *Systematic Review* is obvious, though unsurprising given that Ticehurst had shared his manuscript with Witherby prior to its publication.

The taxonomy of the *Phylloscopus* warblers was once again addressed in Charles Vaurie's 1954 'Systematic Notes on Palearctic Birds. No.9. *Sylviinae*: the Genus *Phylloscopus*'. Vaurie did not support Ticehurst's recognition of *kansuensis* either, noting that 'I have examined only one specimen of *kansuensis*, a paratype which I cannot separate with certainty from nominate *proregulus*.' Nor did he recognise *yunnanensis*, making no reference to this proposed subspecies. The number of accepted subspecies therefore remained at four: nominate *proregulus*, *chloronotus*, *simlaensis* and *forresti*.

This quartet of Pallas's Warbler subspecies was reduced further in 1962 with the publication of the next *Phylloscopus* review, Kenneth Williamson's *Guide to the Genus Phylloscopus*, part of his 'Identification for Ringers' series. With *forresti* treated here as a synonym of *chloronotus*, only three subspecies were now recognised: nominate *proregulus* (south-east Siberia, northern Mongolia and north-east China), *chloronotus* (central China and the Himalayas west to Nepal) and *simlaensis* (western Himalayas).

Such disagreements reflected the basic problems with the concept, summed up by Bernard Tucker in 1949 in the pages of *British Birds*:

> The provision of a hard and fast definition by which species can always be distinguished from subspecies has defied all the efforts of taxonomists for the excellent reason that in nature no hard and fast line of separation exists.

There were other sceptics too, the prominent ornithologist David Lack remarking that:

> It is simpler and more accurate to describe subspecific variation in terms of geographic trends, and to omit altogether the tyranny of subspecific names.

Nevertheless, despite the ongoing debates around subspecies, global taxonomy at the species level continued to be relatively stable. Some subspecies were recategorised as full species, thereby returning them to their nineteenth century status, but most subspecies continued to be accepted as just that, and the upward drift in the number of recognised species remained slow. From the approximately 8,600 bird species recognised in 1946, the total in 1980 had risen to only around 9,000.

Plate 12. Lemon-rumped Warbler (*Arun Singh*)

However, the late twentieth century saw new challenges to this stability. Since 1942 most avian classifications had been based on Ernst Mayr's 'Biological Species Concept' (BSC), first proposed in his *Systematics and the Origin of Species*. Mayr's 'new systematics' represented a departure from traditional approaches, under which obscure morphological characters had been used to define species, to a more holistic approach which considered species as broader biological entities. Mayr defined species as 'groups of actually or potentially interbreeding natural populations, which are reproductively isolated from other such groups'.

This concept worked well with taxa which actually did come into direct contact with each other (i.e. which were 'sympatric') as their degree of isolation could be firmly established. However, taxa which did not come into direct contact (i.e. which were 'allopatric') could not be subjected to the same test of reproductive incompatibility. Defining a species under these circumstances therefore required a subjective judgment to be made.

In the 1980s a rival idea - the 'Phylogenetic Species Concept' (PSC) - was proposed. This asserted a species to be an irreducible group whose members were descended from a common ancestor and which all possessed a combination of certain defining traits. Under this concept all 'diagnosably distinct' taxa, many of which were currently treated as subspecies, would be regarded as full species whilst taxa which were not diagnosably distinct would be regarded simply as variation within a monotypic species. Of course this also required a subjective judgment to be made, in this case over what constituted diagnosability.

The consequence of adopting the PSC would naturally be the end of the subspecies concept and a dramatic increase in the number of recognised species, effectively turning the clock back to the nineteenth century. Despite attracting some support, therefore, the PSC has not gained widespread acceptance and today most classifications still adopt some interpretation of the BSC, though often with a tolerance of hybridisation where this remains limited and does not result in the fusing of the two taxa concerned.

There were other challenges too. Irrespective of one's preferred species concept, new categories of taxonomic evidence were increasingly available. The 1980s brought a new realisation that vocalisations could constitute strong pre-mating isolating mechanisms and could therefore play an important role in systematics. As a result, allopatric taxa which were morphologically very similar but which had distinctive songs and/or calls were increasingly recognised as potential or actual species rather than subspecies. The number of 'new' species therefore began to grow.

In this new area of study, the *Phylloscopus* warblers formed the classic case study. This genus had always been renowned for its poor morphological differentiation, its species usually differing most clearly by their songs. This had been recognised two centuries earlier by Gilbert White who had famously distinguished between the Willow Warbler, Chiffchaff and Wood Warbler in the beech hangers above Selborne, noting to his correspondent Thomas Pennant that 'I have now, past dispute, made out three distinct species of the willow-wrens (*motacillæ trochili*) which constantly and invariably use distinct notes.'

Similar conclusions had also been reached by William Brooks in India. Writing in *The Ibis* in 1894 he noted that 'Four *Phylloscopi* of similar coloration - *P. superciliosus, P. humii, P. subviridis and P. proregulus* - have very distinct voices. I could be sure of recognizing any one of them by note alone, before shooting it.'

Such knowledge had not travelled well down the generations, however. As recently as 1955 Horace Alexander had noted in *British Birds* that 'W. E. Brooks, who worked on the group in India in the 1870's, convinced himself that each species or race had a distinct call-note. My own experience in recent years leads me to doubt this.'

The significance of songs and calls in *Phylloscopus* taxonomy was revisited by Steve Madge in a letter to *British Birds* in 1985. Drawing on his experience in parts of the former Soviet Union, the Himalayas and China - the 'hot-bed of *Phylloscopus* evolution' - he notes not only that the currently recognised species possess distinct vocalisations but also that marked vocal differences exist *within* the boundaries of some species. He continues:

> Clearly we are on the verge of either splitting many more forms of *Phylloscopus* on song differences or lumping some on discovering that vocalisations vary so much as to render conventional tools of systematics of little use within this complex genus.

Despite such caution, however, the value of vocalisations in *Phylloscopus* taxonomy was soon widely accepted, a view encouraged by the results from 'playback' experiments. Despite the morphological similarities within the genus, it appeared that multiple 'cryptic species' were involved.

Amongst the first species to come under scrutiny was the Pallas's Warbler. As early as 1980 Jochen Martens had highlighted distinct differences in territorial song between nominate *proregulus* in Siberia and the geographically well separated *simlaensis* in the western Himalayas. In 1990 Per Alström and Urban Olsson showed that both *simlaensis* and *chloronotus* were vocally distinct from nominate *proregulus* and should therefore be treated together as a full species - '*Phylloscopus chloronotus*', or the 'Lemon-rumped Warbler' - with two subspecies: nominate *chloronotus* in China and the eastern Himalayas and *simlaensis* in the western Himalayas. As a consequence, *Phylloscopus proregulus* - the Pallas's Warbler - would become a monotypic species.

In 1992-93 a number of observers, including Alström and Olsson, found some *Phylloscopus* warblers in Gansu Province which, although apparently identical in their appearance to *Phylloscopus chloronotus*, had very different songs and calls both from that species and from *Phylloscopus proregulus*. They concluded that these birds were *kanusuensis*, the taxon first described by Meise in 1933, initially regarded as a subspecies of *proregulus* but subsequently considered invalid.

A 1997 paper by Alström, Olsson and Peter Colston went on to propose not only that *kansuensis* was a legitimate taxon but that it was specifically distinct too, naming it '*Phylloscopus kansuensis*', or the 'Gansu Leaf Warbler'. Its tiny breeding range in Gansu and Qinghai lay close to that of *Phylloscopus chloronotus* but there was no evidence of overlap or hybridisation. Furthermore, unlike the other conifer-dwelling members of the complex, it appeared to favour deciduous forest.

In parallel with these developments came rapid advances in molecular genetics. These new insights revolutionised avian taxonomy, particularly at the family level, but were also used increasingly to infer limits at the species level. The first technique to be developed involved DNA hybridisation, separating the DNA strands from two species and forming artificial 'hybrid' molecules containing a strand from each. The difference between the two species was then judged by observing how much heat was required to separate the two strands. These techniques, pioneered by Charles Sibley working at first with Jon Ahlquist and later with Burt Monroe, led to a wholesale review of avian systematics.

Subsequent work focused on studying the mitochondrial DNA (mtDNA) present in the ovum and passed down from generation to generation through the female line. The technique compared the sequence of the cytochrome *b* nucleotide from two or more taxa and looked for the percentage divergence.

There were, however, difficulties in interpreting genetic evidence. It was, it was soon realised, no 'silver bullet'. Some morphologically very different taxa proved to have essentially identical DNA whilst deep genetic divides were found within other apparently uniform taxa. Furthermore, large overlaps in genetic distance were found between some taxa currently recognised as species and some recognised as subspecies. The relationship between genetic distance and species status, and therefore its role in taxonomy, had yet to be fully elucidated.

Taxonomists now had multiple strands of evidence to consider, not just morphology, behaviour and ecology but also vocalisations and genetics. Where these lines of evidence all pointed in the same direction they created a powerful case for taxonomic reappraisal. However, this was not always the case and where the evidence offered contradictory clues the taxonomist was left in something of a quandary.

Nevertheless, avian taxonomy quickly erupted in a proliferation of new lists, avifaunas and handbooks in which more and more subspecies were elevated to full species status. The *Phylloscopus* warblers were again the test-bed for these new approaches and their application led to a further revision of their systematics. In Asia alone, the 36 species recognised in the 1980s have now grown to around fifty.

In respect of the Pallas's Warbler group, the first genetic studies confirmed the conclusions reached from the vocal studies, and the three proposed new species became widely recognised as such. In 2004 Martens published the results of a combined vocal and genetic study of the group. He confirmed that all three species were vocally and genetically distinct, their DNA differing by between 3.1% and 4.6%, suggesting a separation of between 1.7 and 3.2 million years.

Martens also identified a fourth species within what he now termed the Pallas's Warbler 'superspecies'. The new addition was the south-western Chinese population, described by Rothschild in 1918 as *forresti* but regarded as invalid by later authors. This too was now proposed as a full species - '*Phylloscopus forresti*', or the 'Sichuan Leaf Warbler' - with

Phylloscopus chloronotus therefore redefined, now referring only to birds from the Himalayas.

The 'missing' subspecies, the briefly-recognised *yunnanesis* of La Touche, also proved to be both a valid taxon and a species in its own right - '*Phylloscopus yunnanensis*', or the 'Chinese Leaf Warbler' - breeding extensively in inland China and overlapping in range with both *Phylloscopus forresti* and *Phylloscopus kansuensis*. This taxon was rediscovered by Alström and others and described in 1992 as a new species - '*Phylloscopus sichuanensis*' - though it was later established to be the long-forgotten *yunnanensis*. This species is closely related and morphologically similar to *Phylloscopus forresti* and *Phylloscopus kansuensis* but its weak central crown stripe and lack of dark bases to the flight feathers as well as significant vocal and genetic differences point to it being a 'sister species' within a broader species group and not a member of the Pallas's Warbler superspecies.

With the exception of *Phylloscopus forresti*, all these new species are now recognised by all the leading world taxonomic authorities. However, 2014 brought further taxonomic instability with the proposal to remove the tiny wing-barred leaf warblers, including the Pallas's Warbler superspecies, from their long-standing home in the genus *Phylloscopus* and reassign them to *Abrornis*, the genus first described by the Grays in 1847.

The taxonomy of the Pallas's Warbler has therefore been both long and tortuous and has, in some respects, come full circle. For example, the subspecies identified in the early years of the twentieth century but subsequently largely dismissed and forgotten have now been resurrected, confirmed not only as valid taxa but as full species in their own right. There are still questions, however. The precise location of the contact zones between the newly-defined Sino-Himalayan species and the extent of hybridisation (if any) between them remain undetermined.

Today taxonomy is perhaps more hotly debated than ever. Arguments rage not just over the relative merits of the various categories of evidence but also over competing species concepts. The taxonomic environment has changed too, with a new 'democracy' at play. Today's pronouncements are no longer made exclusively by museum taxonomists or by 'competent systematists' but by people from a whole host of disciplines, both professional and amateur. Field ornithologists, sound recordists, geneticists and birdwatchers all claim an opinion and these are endlessly discussed in both peer-reviewed and popular journals, on internet fora and on social media.

There are wider stakeholders too, for example governments, conservation bodies and records committees who need to adjust their legislative, protection and recording regimes according to prevailing thinking. Taxonomy has therefore become a highly political as well as a natural science.

Wherever such debates may lead, however, one thing is certain. 'Siberia's sprite' will remain our constant companion, testing our ideas and theories as well as our tools and techniques, a continuing witness to our fascinations and desires.

BIBLIOGRAPHY

Alerstam, T. 1990. *Bird Migration*. Cambridge University Press.

Alexander, H. G. 1955. Field-notes on some Asian Leaf-Warblers. *British Birds* 48: 293-299.

Alström, P. & Olsson, U. 1990. Taxonomy of the *Phylloscopus proregulus* complex. *Bulletin of the British Ornithologists' Club* 110: 38-43.

Alström, P. *et al.* 1997. Re-evaluation of the taxonomic status of *Phylloscopus proregulus kansuensis* Meise. *Bulletin of the British Ornithologists' Club* 117: 177-193.

Alström, P. 2001. The Use of Sounds in Bird Systematics. Introductory Research Essay No. 2. Uppsala.

Alström, P. 2006. Species concepts and their application: insights from the genera *Seicercus* and *Phylloscopus*. *Acta Zoologica Sinica* 52 (Supplement): 429-434.

Archer, M., Grantham, M., Howlett, P. & Stansfield, S. 2010. *Bird Observatories of Britain and Ireland*. Poyser, London.

Arnold, E. C. 1947. *Memories of Cley*. Baskerville Press, Eastbourne.

Baker, K. 1977. Westward Vagrancy of Siberian Passerines in Autumn 1975. *Bird Study* 24: 233-242.

Baker, J. K. & Catley, G. P. 1987. Yellow-browed Warblers in Britain and Ireland, 1968-85. *British Birds* 80: 93-109.

Bell, D. G. 1962. Pallas's Warbler in Co. Durham. *British Birds* 56: 112-113.

Benson, S. V. 1937. *The Observer's Book of Birds*. Frederick Warne.

Beolens, B. & Watkins, M. 2003. *Whose Bird? Men and women commemorated in the common names of birds*. Helm, London.

Biddulph, J. 1882. On the Birds of Gilgit. *The Ibis* 24: 266-290.

Birkhead, T., Wimpenny, J & Montgomerie, B. 2014. *Ten Thousand Birds: Ornithology since Darwin*. Princeton University Press, Princeton and Oxford.

Blyth, E. 1866. The Ornithology of India. *The Ibis* 8: 225-258.

Bonhomme, B. 1962. *Russian Exploration, from Siberia to Space: A History*. McFarland & Company, Inc., Jefferson, North Carolina.

Borrer, C. 2000. The Pallas's Warbler in Norfolk: a new British bird. *Birding World* 13: 126-127.

Brooks, W. E. 1872. 'On the breeding of *Reguloides superciliosus, Reguloides proregulus, Reguloides occipitalis* and *Phylloscopus tytleri*.' *The Ibis* 14:24-31.

Brooks, W. E. 1894. A few Observations on some Species of *Phylloscopus*. *The Ibis* 36: 261-268.

Busby, J. 1982. *The Living Birds of Eric Ennion*. Victor Gollancz Ltd, London.

Busby, J. 1986. *Drawing Birds*. RSPB, Sandy, Beds.

Cambridge Bird Club. 1958. Pallas's Warbler in Norfolk. *British Birds* 51: 197.

Catley, G. P. 1992. Identification pitfalls and assessment problems (13. Pallas's Warbler). *British Birds* 85: 490-494.

Clarke, R. B., Coath, M., Johns, R. J. and Jones, D. B. D. 1961. Pallas's Warbler in Essex. *British Birds* 54: 73-74.

Clarke, W. E. 1912. *Studies in Bird Migration*. Oliver & Boyd, Edinburgh.

Collar, N. J. 2004. Pioneers of Asian ornithology: Robert Swinhoe. *BirdingASIA* 1: 49-53.

Collar, N. 2013. A species is whatever I say it is. *British Birds* 106: 130-142.

Collinson, M. 2006. Splitting headaches? Recent taxonomic changes affecting the British and Western Palearctic lists. *British Birds* 99: 306-323.

Cottridge, D. & Vinicombe, K. 1997. *Rare Birds in Britain & Ireland: A Photographic Record*. Collins.

Coues, E. 1872. *Key to North American Birds*. Dodd and Mead, New York.

Coward, T. A. 1920-25. *The Birds of the British Isles and their Eggs*. Frederick Warne, London.

Cross, A. 2014. *In the Land of the Romanovs: An Annotated Bibliography of First-hand English-language Accounts of the Russian Empire (1613-1917)*. Open Book Publishers, Cambridge.

David, A. *1875 Journal de mon troisième voyage d'exploration dans l'empire Chinois*. Hachette et cie, Paris.

David, A. & Oustalet, E. 1877. *Les Oiseaux de la Chine*. Masson, Paris.

Davidson, J. 1898. A Short Trip to Kashmir. *The Ibis* 40: 1-42.

De Juana, E. 2008. Where do Pallas's and Yellow-browed Warblers go after visiting Northwest Europe in Autumn? An Iberian Perspective. *Ardeola* 55: 179-192.

Dennis, R. H. 1967. Pallas's Warbler at Fair Isle: a new Scottish bird. *Scottish Birds* 4: 454.

Dickinson, E. C. & Walters, M. Systematic notes on Asian birds. 53. The authorship and date of publication of the "Catalogue of the Specimens and Drawings of Mammalia and Birds of Nepal and Thibet presented by B. H. Hodgson, Esq. to the British Museum". *Zool. Med. Leiden* 80-5 (5), 21.xii.2006: 137-153.

Dillon, M. 2010. *China: A Modern History*. I. B. Tauris & Co., London.

Dixon, S. (ed.). 2010. *Personality and Place in Russian Culture*. University College London.

Dresser, H. E. 1895-96. *Supplement to a History of the Birds of Europe*. London.

Dresser, H. E. 1897. Notes on Pallas's Willow Warbler and some other rare European warblers. *Transactions of the Norfolk & Norwich Naturalists' Society* 6: 280-290.

Durman, R. (ed.). 1976. *Bird Observatories in Britain and Ireland*. T. & A. D. Poyser Ltd., Berkhamsted.

Dymond, J. N. & the Rarities Committee. 1976. Report on rare birds in Great Britain in 1975. *British Birds* 69: 321-368.

Elkins, N. 1983. *Weather and Bird Behaviour*. T. & A. D. Poyser Ltd., Calton.

Elkins, N. 1991. Eastern vagrants in Britain in autumn 1988. *British Birds* 84: 402-404.

Ennion, E. A. R. 1952. Pallas's Warbler at Monks' House, Northumberland. *British Birds* 45: 258-260.

Ennion, E. A. R. 1959. *The House on the Shore: The Story of Monk's House Bird Observatory*. Routledge & Kegan Paul Ltd., London.

Fisher, J. 1966. *The Shell Bird Book*. Ebury Press & Michael Joseph, London.

Fitter, R. S. R. & Richardson, R. A. 1952. *Collins Pocket Guide to British Birds*. Collins, London.

Fraser, P. A. & Ryan, J. F. 1994. Scarce migrants in Britain and Ireland Part 2: Numbers during 1986-92: gulls to passerines. *British Birds* 87: 605-612.

Fraser, P. A., Lansdown, P. G. & Rogers, M. J. 1997. Report on scarce migrant birds in Britain in 1995. *British Birds* 90: 413-439.

Fraser, P. A. & Rogers, M. J. 2006. Report on scarce migrant birds in Britain in 2003 Part 2: Short-toed Lark to Little Bunting. *British Birds* 99: 129–147.

Gätke, H. 1895. *Heligoland as an Ornithological Observatory*. David Douglas, Edinburgh.

Gilroy, J. & Lees, A. 2003. Vagrancy theories: are autumn vagrants really reverse migrants? *British Birds* 96: 427-438.

Gilroy, J. *et al.* 2016. Migratory diversity predicts population declines in birds. *Ecology Letters.*

Gmelin, J. G. 1752. *Reise durch Sibirien von dem Jahr 1733 bis 1743.* Göttingen, Verlegts Abram Vandenhoecks seel., Wittwe.

Gmelin, J. G. 1747-49. *Flora Sibirica sive Historia plantarum Sibiriae*. Ex Typographia Academiae Scientiarum.

Gould, J. 1837. *Birds of Europe*. London.

Gould, J. 1863. *Birds of Asia*. London.

Gray, G. R. 1844-49. *The Genera of Birds*. Longman, Brown, Green, and Longmans, London.

Gray, J. E. 1846. *Catalogue of the specimens and drawings of Mammalia and birds of Nepal and Thibet presented by B. H. Hodgson Esq. to the British Museum*. British Museum, London.

Gray, J. E. 1863. *Catalogue of the specimens and drawings of Mammalia and birds of Nepal and Tibet presented by B. H. Hodgson Esq. to the British Museum*. 2nd ed. London.

Hammond, N. 1986. *Twentieth Century Wildlife Artists*. Helm, London.

Hammond, N. 1998. *Modern Wildlife Painting*. Yale University Press, New Haven and London.

Harber, D. D. & the Rarities Committee. 1966. Report on rare birds in Great Britain in 1965. *British Birds* 59: 280-305.

Harle, D. F. 1959. Pallas's Warbler in Kent. *British Birds* 52: 317-318.

Hartert, E., Jourdain, F. C. R., Ticehurst, N. F. & Witherby, H. F. 1912. *A Hand-List of British Birds*. Witherby & Co., London.

Haywood, A. J. 2010. *Siberia: A Cultural History*. Signal Books, Oxford.

Heawood, E. A. 1912. *History of Geographical Discovery in the Seventeenth and Eighteenth Centuries*. Cambridge University Press.

Hemming, F. 1951. Date of publication of Pallas's 'Zoographia Rosso-Asiatica'. *The Ibis* 93: 316-321.

Hodgson, B. H. 1843. Catalogue of Nepalese birds presented to the Asiatic Society, duly named and classified by the Donor [and revised by the Society's Curator]. *J. Asiatic Soc. Bengal* XII 136: 301-313.

Howey, D. H. & Bell, M. 1985. Pallas's Warblers and other migrants in Britain and Ireland in October 1982. *British Birds* 78: 381-392.

Hume, A. O. 1879. *List of the Birds of India.*

Hume, A. O. 1889. *The Nests and Eggs of Indian Birds.* R. H. Porter, London.

Jerdon, T. C. 1863. *The Birds of India.* T. C. Jerdon.

Jones, R. T. 2014. *Empire of Extinction: Russians and the North Pacific's Strange Beasts of the Sea, 1741-1867.* Oxford University Press.

Jonsson, L. 1992. *Birds of Europe.* Helm, London.

Kershaw, J. C. 1904. List of the Birds of the Quangtung Coast, China. *The Ibis* 46: 235-248.

La Touche, J. D. D. 1892. On Birds Collected or Observed in the Vicinity of Foochow and Swatow in South-eastern China. *The Ibis* 34: 400-430.

La Touche, J. D. D. 1899. Notes on the Birds of North-west Fokhien. *The Ibis* 41: 169-210.

La Touche, J. D. D. 1906. Field notes on the Birds of Chinkiang, Lower Yangtse Basin - Part 1. *The Ibis* 48: 427-450.

La Touche, J. D. D. 1914. The spring migration at Chinwangtao in north-east Chihli. *The Ibis* 56: 560-586.

La Touche, J. D. D. 1920. Notes on the Birds of North-east Chihli, in North China. *The Ibis* 62: 629-671.

La Touche, J. D. D. 1923. On the Birds of South-East Yunnan - Part 2. *The Ibis* 65: 369-414.

La Touche, J. D. D. 1925-34. *A Handbook of the Birds of Eastern China*. Taylor & Francis, London.

Lansdell, H. 1882. *Through Siberia*. Arno Press, New York.

Lehman, P. E. & Rosenberg, G. H. 2007. First North American record of Pallas's Warbler (*Phylloscopus proregulus*) at Gambell, Alaska. *North American Birds* 61: 4-8.

Lilford, T. 1885-97. *Coloured Figures of the Birds of the British Islands*. R. H. Porter, London.

Maclean, N., Collinson, M. & Newell, R. G. 2005. Taxonomy for birders: A beginner's guide to DNA and species problems. *British Birds* 98: 512-537.

Madge, S. C. 1985. Vocalisations and *Phylloscopus* taxonomy. *British Birds* 78: 199.

Martens, J., Tietze, D. T., Eck, S. & Veith, M. 2004. Radiation and species limits in the Asian Pallas's warbler complex (*Phylloscopus proregulus s.l.*). *Journal of Ornithology* 145: 206-222.

Martens, J. 2010. A preliminary review of the leaf warbler genera *Phylloscopus* and *Seicercus*. *Brit. Orn. Club Occas. Publs* 5: 41–116.

Matthiessen, P. 1992. *Baikal: Sacred Sea of Siberia*. Sierra Club Books, San Francisco.

Mayr, E. 1942. *Systematics and the Origin of Species*. Columbia University Press.

Mearns, B. & R. 1998. *The Bird Collectors*. Academic Press, London.

Mlíkovský, J. 2007. Types of birds in the collections of the Museum and Institute of Zoology, Polish Academy of Sciences, Warszawa, Poland. Part 2: Asian birds. *Journal of the National Museum (Prague), Natural History Series* Vol. 176: 33-79.

Morris, Rev. F. O. 1851-57. *A History of British Birds*. Groombridge and Sons, London.

Moss, S. 2004. *A Social History of Birdwatching*. Aurum Press Ltd., London.

Naumann, J. A. 1897. *Naturgeshichte der Vögel Mitteleuropas*. Gera-Untermhaus, F. E. Köhler.

Oates, E. W. 1889. *The Fauna of British India: Birds Vol I*. Taylor and Francis, London.

Pallas, P. S. *Travels into Siberia and Tartary, provinces of the Russian empire* (in Vols 2-4 of Trusler, J. 1788-89. *The habitable world described*).

Pallas, P. S. 1811. *Zoographia Rosso-Asiatica*.

Pashley, H. N. 1925. *Notes on the Birds of Cley*. Witherby, London.

Peterson, R. T. *et al.* 1974. *A Field Guide to the Birds of Britain and Europe*. Collins, London.

Phillips, J. 2000. Autumn vagrancy: "Reverse migration" and migratory orientation. *Ringing & Migration* 20: 35-38.

Pleske, T. 1889-92. *Ornithographia Rossica*. St. Petersburg.

Power, F. D. 1885. Ornithological Notes at Cley and Blakeney September 3rd to 19th 1884. *Transactions of the Norfolk & Norwich Naturalists' Society* 4: 36-43.

Przewalski, N. 1876. *Mongolia, the Tangut Country and the Solitudes of Northern Tibet*. S. Low, Marston, Searle, & Rivington, London.

Pyman, G. A. 1960. Report on rare birds in Great Britain and Ireland in 1958. *British Birds* 54: 153-173.

Rabøl, J. 1969. Reversed migration as the cause of westward vagrancy by four *Phylloscopus* warblers. *British Birds* 62: 89-92.

Rabøl, J. 1976. The orientation of Pallas's Warblers in Europe. *Dansk Ornitologisk Forenings Tidsskrift* 70: 6-16.

Radde, G. 1862-63. *Reisen im Süden von Ost-Sibirien in den Jahren 1855-59*.

Ravenstein, E. G. 1861. *The Russians on the Amur*. Trübner & Co., London.

Rheindt, F. E. 2006. Splits galore: the revolution in Asian leaf warbler systematics. *BirdingAsia* 5: 25-39.

Ridgway, R. 1881. *Nomenclature of North American Birds*. Washington Govt. Print. Off.

Rogers, M. J. & the Rarities Committee. 1983. Report on rare birds in Great Britain in 1982. *British Birds* 76: 476-529.

Rooke, K. B. 1966. The orientation of vagrant Pallas's Warblers. *XIV Int. Orn. Congr. Abstracts*.

Sangster, G. *et al.* 2005. Taxonomic recommendations for British Birds: third report. *Ibis* 147: 821-826.

Saunders, H. 1899. *An Illustrated Manual of British Birds*. Gurney and Jackson, London.

Scott, R. E. 1964. Pallas's Warblers in Britain in 1963. *British Birds* 57: 508-513.

Seago, M. (ed.). 1964. *Norfolk Bird & Mammal Report 1963*. Norfolk and Norwich Naturalists' Society, Norwich.

Seebohm H. 1877. Supplementary Notes on the Ornithology of Heligoland. *The Ibis* 19: 156-165.

Seebohm, H. 1877. On the *Phylloscopi* or Willow-Warblers. *The Ibis* 19: 66-108.

Seebohm, H. 1879. Remarks on certain points in Ornithological Nomenclature. *The Ibis* 21: 428-437.

Seebohm, H. 1880. *Siberia in Europe: a visit to the valley of the Petchora, in north-east Europe*. J. Murray, London.

Seebohm, H. 1892. List of the Birds of Heligoland as recorded by Heinrich Gätke. *The Ibis* 34: 1-32.

Seebohm, H. 1901. *The birds of Siberia; a record of a naturalist's visits to the valleys of the Petchora and Yenesei*. J. Murray, London.

Sharrock, J. T. R. & Preston, K. 1969. Pallas's Warbler on Cape Clear Island: A Bird New to Ireland. *The Irish Naturalists' Journal* 16: 173-174.

Smith, F. R. & the Rarities Committee. 1969. Report on rare birds in Great Britain in 1968. *British Birds* 62: 457-492.

Smith, F. R. & the Rarities Committee. 1971. Report on rare birds in Great Britain in 1970. *British Birds* 64: 339-371.

Smith, F. R. & the Rarities Committee. 1975. Report on rare birds in Great Britain in 1974. *British Birds* 68: 306-338.

Stoddart, A. M. & Joyner, S. C. 2005. *The Birds of Blakeney Point*. Wren Publishing, Sheringham.

Stoddart, A. M. 2011. *Shifting Sands: Blakeney Point and the Environmental Imagination*. Privately published.

Strickland, H. E. 1842. *Series of Propositions for rendering the Nomenclature of Zoology uniform and permanent*. Report to the British Association for the Advancement of Science.

Styan, F. W. 1887. On a Collection of Birds from Foochow. *The Ibis* 29: 215-234.

Styan, F. W. 1891. On the Birds of the Lower Yangtse Basin - Part 1. *The Ibis* 33: 316-359.

Swinhoe, R. 1860. The ornithology of Amoy (China). *The Ibis* 2: 45-68.

Swinhoe, R. 1861. Notes on the ornithology of Hongkong, Macao, and Canton, made during the latter end of February, March, April, and the beginning of May, 1860. *The Ibis* 3: 23-57.

Swinhoe, R. 1861. Notes on Ornithology taken between Tahoo and Peking, in the neighbourhood of the Peiho River, Province of Chelee, North China, from August to December 1860. *The Ibis* 3: 328-345.

Swinhoe, R. 1862. Ornithological Ramble in Foochow in December 1861. *The Ibis* 4: 253-265.

Swinhoe, R. 1863. Catalogue of the birds of China. *Proceedings of the Zoological Society of London*. 17: 259-338.

Swinhoe, R. 1866. A Voice on Ornithology from Formosa. *The Ibis* 8: 129-138.

Swinhoe, R. 1867. Jottings on Birds from my Amoy Journal. *The Ibis* 9: 226-237.

Swinhoe, R. 1870. On the ornithology of Hainan. *The Ibis* 12: 77-97.

Styan, F. 1891. List of the Birds of the Lower Yangtze Basin - Part 1. *The Ibis* 33: 316-359.

Taczanowski, L. 1872. Bericht über die ornithologischen Untersuchungen des Dr. Dybowski in Ost-Sibirien. *Journal für Ornithologie* 119: 340-366.

Taylor, M. 2002. *Guardian Spirit of the East Bank: A Celebration of the Life of R. A. Richardson*. Wren Publishing, Sheringham.

Thorburn, A. 1915-16. *British Birds*. Longmans, Green and Co., London.

Thorup, K. 1998. Vagrancy of Yellow-browed Warbler and Pallas's Warbler in north-west Europe: Misorientation on great circles? *Ringing & Migration* 19: 7-12.

Thorup, K. 2004. Reverse migration as a cause of vagrancy. *Bird Study* 51: 228-238.

Thubron, C. 1999. *In Siberia*. Chatto & Windus, London.

Tucker, B. W. 1949. Species and subspecies: a review for general ornithologists. *British Birds* 42: 129-134, 161-174, 193-205.

Vaurie, C. 1954. Systematic Notes on Palearctic Birds No. 9. *Sylviinae*: the Genus *Phylloscopus*. *American Museum Novitates* 1685: 1-23.

Von Middendorff, A. T. 1853. *Reise in den äußersten Norden und Osten Sibiriens während der Jähre 1843 und 1844*.

Von Pelzeln, 1868. On the species of birds collected by Dr. Stoliczka in Thibet and the Himalayas. *Ibis* 10: 302-321.

Wallace, D. I. M. 1979. *Discover Birds*. Whizzard Press/Andre Deutsch.

Wallace, D. I. M. 2004. *Beguiled by Birds*. Christopher Helm, London.

Walters, M. 2003. *A Concise History of Ornithology*. Yale University Press.

Waterhouse, D. M. 2004. *The Origins of Himalayan Studies: Brian Houghton Hodgson in Nepal and Darjeeling*. RoutledgeCurzon, London and New York.

White, S. & Kehoe, C. 2016. Report on scarce migrant birds in Britain in 2013. *British Birds* 109: 96-121.

Williamson, K. 1962. *Identification for Ringers: The Genus Phylloscopus*. British Trust for Ornithology.

Williamson, K. 1965. *Fair Isle and its Birds*. Oliver & Boyd, Edinburgh and London.

Wilson, D. 1996. *China, the Big Tiger: A Nation Awakes*. Abacus, London.

Witherby, H. F., Jourdain, F. C. R., Ticehurst, N. F. & Tucker, B. W. 1938-41. *The Handbook of British Birds*. Witherby, London.

Wolstenholme, P. H. G., Butterworth, J. M. & Chislett, R. 1961. Pallas's Warbler in Yorkshire. *British Birds* 54: 364-365.

Yarrell, W. 1843. *A History of British Birds*. John van Voorst, London.

Ziegler, D. 2015. *Black Dragon River: A Journey down the Amur River at the Borderlands of Empires*. Penguin Press, New York.

INDEX OF PROPER NAMES

Academy of Sciences 9, 15, 20-22
Aeuckens, Claus 56-57
Africa 113, 129
Africa, East 126
Ahlquist, Jon 138
Aigun, Treaty of 20
Alashan Desert 47
Alaska 7, 22, 127
Alerstam, Thomas 126
Alexander I 20
Alexander, Horace 95, 136
Alström, Per 137, 140
Altai Mountains 10, 47
Alt-Tsuruchaitui 26
Altyn Tag 47
America 6
America, North 81, 117
America, South 113
Amur, River 5, 6, 14, 20-22, 26-27, 56

Amur Territory 43
Anderby 101
Angara River 5
Arctic 58
Argun 7
Argun, River 14, 26
Arnold, E. C. 65-67
Ashworth, Rev. E. H. 66
Asia 29, 54, 56-57, 121, 124, 139
Asia, Central 127
Askold Island 23, 26
Assam 32
Australia 113

Baikal, Lake 5, 6-7, 10, 14, 23, 25, 27
Baikal Region 6, 23, 25-27
Bailey, J. A. 100
Baker, Kevin 123, 124
Bamburgh 91
Baoxing 48
Baranovskij 26
Bardsey 88
Baxter, Evelyn 87, 89
Beijing 41, 45, 48-49
Bell, M. 123
Benson, S. Vere 115
Bering Island 7
Bering, Vitus 6-7
Berlin 8, 46, 79
Bhagirathi, River 35
Bhaironghati 36
Bhutan 32, 38
Biddulph, Col. John 37
Biological Species Concept 134
BirdLife International 140
Birdline 105
Birmingham 71

Birmingham Museum 71
Blackcap 130
Blackmoorfoot Reservoir 103
Black Sea 15, 124
Blakeney 65
Blakeney Point 63, 65, 71, 80, 93, 95-96, 112
Bluetail, Red-flanked 13, 117
Bluethroat 59, 65, 91
Blyth, Edward 30-31, 76, 81
Bohai, Gulf of 46
Bolshoy Kamen 26
Borrer, Clifford 66
Brambling 92
Brandt, Johann 20
Brent, William 66
Brisson, Mathurin 8
Britain 29, 62-63, 67, 80, 90, 93, 102, 111, 123, 128-130
British Association for the Advancement of Science 78-79
British Birds Rarities Committee 98
British Consular Service 40
British Museum 31, 34, 60, 112-113, 131
British Ornithologists' Union 63
British Trust for Ornithology 88
Broads, The 65
Brooks, William 35-37, 136
Buffon, Comte de 9
Bunting, Black-faced 14
Bunting, Godlewski's 23
Bunting, Jankowski's 24
Bunting, Little 14, 57, 59
Bunting, Pallas's Reed 16
Bunting, Rustic 14
Bunting, Yellow-browed 14, 102
Burma 32
Busby, John 116
Bushchat, Hodgson's 32
Bushchat, Jerdon's 32

Butterworth, J. M. 99

Calcutta 29
California 20
Cambridge 96
Cambridge Bird Club 96
Cambridgeshire 90
Cape Clear Island 101
Caspian Region 10
Caspian Sea 123
Castleford Museum 71
Catley, Graham 106, 124
Catherine II 9-10, 15, 20
Caucasus 10, 15
Chamba 37
Chengdu 48
Chepstow 71
Chiffchaff 67, 136
Chiffchaff, Siberian 112
Chilok, River 12
China 6, 12-13, 20-21, 32, 37-40, 44-47, 49, 62, 121, 131-133, 136-137, 139-140
Chita 6, 14, 23, 25
Chongqing 40, 48
Clarke, William Eagle 87, 89
Clements 140
Cley-next-the-Sea 64-66, 68, 71, 88, 95, 117
Cock, Captain 35-37
Colston, Peter 137
Commander Islands 7, 26
Connop, Ernest 71
Connops 66
Copeland 88
Cottridge, David 126
County Durham 100
Courser, Jerdon's 32
Cordeaux, John 58, 86-87

Cormorant, Pallas's 16
Corncrake 59
Cornell 140
Coues, Elliott 81-82
County Cork 101
Coward, T. A. 115
Crimea 15
Croatia 51
Customs Service 45
Cutbill, J. L. 96

Dalmatia 51, 62
Darasun 25
Darjeeling 29
Darwin, Charles 51
David, Père Armand 48
Davidson, J. 37
Decembrists 23
Dehradun 32, 38
De Juana, Eduardo 129
Dharali 36
Dauria 14, 16
Denmark 126
Dipper, Pallas's 16
Dähn, Lorenz 57
Dörries, Friedrich and Heinrich 26
Dove, Collared 108
Dresser, Henry 60-61, 68-69, 76-77, 79, 112, 114
'Duchess' 66, 68
Dungeness 88
Dybowski, Benedykt 22-26, 47, 54, 57, 60-61, 75, 104, 112

Eastbourne College 65
East India Company 29, 31-32
East Siberia Expedition 21
Eddystone Lighthouse 87
Eider, Steller's 7

Elkins, Norman 123
England 8, 40, 87, 122, 125
Enlightenment, The 8, 73
Ennion, Eric 90-93, 115-116
Essex 99
Europe 9, 26, 51-52, 57, 62, 65, 81, 122, 124, 126-129
Europe, Central 130

Fair Isle 87-90, 100, 102, 104
Farne Islands 91
Feldegg, Baron Cristoph 51-52, 109
Finsch, Otto 75
Firecrest 119
Firethroat 48
First War 85
Fish Eagle, Pallas's 16
Fitter, Richard 118
Flannan Isles 87
Flatford Mill 90
Flycatcher, Collared 126
Flycatcher, Pied 89-90
Flycatcher, Red-breasted 67
Forrest, George 131
Forth, Firth of 88
France 20, 122
Fujian Province 45
Fuzhou 40, 44-45

Galapagos 51
Gangadgir 37
Gangotri 36
Gansu Province 48, 132, 137-138
Gätke, Heinrich 52-57, 59, 76, 89, 96, 122
Germany 20, 52-53
Gibraltar Point 88
Gilgit 36, 132
Gilroy, James 128

Gmelin, Johann 6-10
Gmelin, Samuel 10
Gobi Desert 47, 48, 124
Godlewski, Wiktor 22-23
Goldcrest 16, 32, 51-52, 68, 74-75, 86, 90, 92, 96-97, 99, 103, 106, 119
Gore Point 96
Gould, Elizabeth 51, 111
Gould, John 31, 40, 51-52, 74, 109-111
Gray, George 31, 75, 140
Gray, John 31, 75, 140
Grönvold, Henrik 113
Ground Jay, Hume's 37
Guadun 45
Guanghzhou 39, 41
Gulag 23
Güldenstädt, Johann 10, 15
Gull, Pallas's 16
Gulmerg 36
Gund 37
Gunn, T. E. 66

Hainan 40, 44
Hancock, John 69, 71
Han River 49
Hart, William 111
Hartert, Ernst 80
Hartlepool 100
Hartley 69
Harvie-Brown, John 86-87
Hazara 38
Hebei 46
Heligoland 52-53, 56, 58-59, 62, 87-89, 92, 96
Henan 49
Hickling 71
Highland 107
Himachal Pradesh 34, 37

Himalayas 31-32, 35, 37-38, 41, 47, 50, 75-76, 80-81, 124, 132, 133, 136-137, 139
Hodgson, Brian 29-32, 35, 51, 75
Holkham 104-105
Holkham Meals 102
Holland 8-9
Hollom, Phil 117
Holme Bird Observatory 118
Holme-next-the-Sea 95-96, 100
Homeyer, Eugen von 57
Hong Kong 39-41, 45
Hoopoe 91
Howard and Moore 140
Howard, Henry 113
Howey, D. H. 123
Hume, Allan Octavian 32-35, 37, 76
Hunter, William 31

Iberian Peninsula 129
India 21, 29-30, 32, 34, 38-39, 131, 136
Indian Civil Service 33
Indian Rebellion 29
Ingoda, River 14, 16, 21, 25, 74
Inner Mongolia 48
International Commission on Zoological Nomenclature 79
International Ornithological Congress 140
Ireland 47, 101, 104-105
Irkutsk 6, 7, 11-12, 25-26
Isle of Wight 100

Jableni-Daba 14
Jackdaw, Daurian 12
Jankowski, Michael 22-23, 26
January Uprising 22
Japan 127
Jardin des Plantes 48
Jerdon, Thomas 32, 36, 81

Jiangsu Province 45
Jiangxi Province 44
Jiujiang 44, 49
Jonsson, Lars 118-119
Jourdain, Francis 80, 115

Kamchatka 7, 22, 26
Kashmir 32, 36-38, 132
Kathmandu 29-30, 32
Katorga system 23
Kayak Island 7
Kent 65, 97, 103
Kentish Knock Lightship 87
Kershaw, John 44
Keulemans, John 111-114
Khanka, Lake 26
Khasi Hills 32, 38
Khentii Mountains 14
Kiev University 21
Koekkoek, Marinus 115
Korea 23
Kotgarh 37
Krasnoyarsk 5, 10, 12
Kullussutajevsk 22
Kultuk 23, 25-26, 60, 112
Kumaon 29
Kunstammer Museum 15
Kyakhta 7, 26

La Touche, John 44-46, 131, 139
Lack, David 133
Lark, Shore 12, 59
Latham, John 8
Lauhukuo 132
Lear, Edward 111
Lees, Alex 128
Leiden 79

Leiden, University of 8
Lena River 5, 7, 14, 27
Lepechin, Ivan 10
Lijiang Range 131
Lilford, Lord 69, 112, 114
Lincolnshire 65, 86, 101
Linnaeus, Carl 9, 73, 78, 80
Lockley, Ronald 88
Lodge, George 113
London 51, 64, 66
Lop Nor Depression 47
Lundy 88
Lysgaht, William 71

Macao 41, 45
Madge, Steve 136
Manipur 38
Markul 21
Martens, Jochen 137, 139
Maximovicz, Karl 22
May, Isle of 88, 90, 103
Mayr, Ernst 134
Meise, Wilhelm 132, 137
Mengzi 131
Messerschmidt, Daniel 6
Michael I 5
Middendorff, Alexander von 21, 75
Molleson, Wladislaw 26
Monal, Chinese 48
Mongolia 7, 14, 47-48, 133
Monks' House 88, 90-92, 96, 115
Monroe, Burt 138
Morris, Rev. Francis 70
Moscow 61
Mountfort, Guy 117
Muraviev, Nikolai 20
Muséum National d'Histoire Naturelle 48

Mussoorie 32
Myanmar 38

Naga Hills 38
Nancy's Café 105
Nanking, Treaty of 39
Napoleon 20
Naumann, Johann 60, 112
Nepal 29-32, 35, 51, 132- 133
Nerchinsk 6
Nerchinsk, Treaty of 6, 20
Neshenka 61
New Holland 47
New World 20
Newton, Alfred 79
Nicholas I 20, 23
Nightingale, Thrush 87
Ningbo 40
Norfolk 64-68, 71, 95, 100-102, 117
Norfolk and Norwich Naturalists' Society 65, 112
North Sea 58, 89-90, 122-123, 127
Northern Isles 89
Northumberland 69, 90
Norwich 101
Nuthatch, Przewalski's 48

Oates, Eugene 37, 76
Ob, River 5
Ocean, Arctic 5, 127
Ocean, Pacific 5, 7, 20, 22, 27, 126
Okhotsk 7
Okhotsk, Sea of 21
Olsson, Urban 137
Onon, River 14
Opium War 39
Orenburg 61-62
Orkney 87

Orlow, Count 10
Ouang-kia-Ouan 49
Oustalet, Emile 50
Ouzel, Ring 59

Pa-ko-Chan 49
Pakistan 37
Pallas, Peter Simon 8-11, 13-16, 21, 52, 74-75
Pamir Mountains 47
Panda, Giant 49
Pangi 37
Paris 48-49, 79
Paul I 20
Pashley, Henry 65, 67, 69, 71
Payn, Col. W. A. 66
Pechora, River 81
Pembrokeshire 88
Pennant, Thomas 8, 9, 15, 136
Peter the Great 6
Peter the Great Bay 23
Peterson, Roger Tory 117, 119
Petrel, Swinhoe's 40
Petrovsk 25
Phalarope, Grey 91
Phillips, John 128
Phylogenetic Species Concept 135
Pinchen, Bob 66, 71
Pipit, Blyth's 31
Pipit, Richard's 54, 59, 87
Pleske, Theodor 26, 48, 61
Plover, Grey 59
Poland 22-23
Portland 88
Power, Fred and George 64-66
'Prince' 66
Protopopen Grove 61
Przewalski, Nikolai 26, 47-48

Prussia, West 21

Qaidam Basin 47
Qinghai Lake 47
Qinghai Province 132, 138
Qinhuangdao 46
Quangtung Coast 44

Rabøl, Jørgen 124
Radde, Gustav 21-22
Ramm, Ted 66, 68, 71, 93
Rarity Records Committee 98, 124
Redstart 67, 89-90
Redstart, Black 91
Redstart, Hodgson's 32
Redstart, Przewalski's 48
Richards, Frank 66
Richardson, Richard 117-118
Richter, Henry 111
Ridgway, Robert 81-82
Rintoul, Leonora
Robin 67, 90, 92
Robin, Swinhoe's 40
Rollesby Hall 71
Romanovs 5
Rooke, K. B. 124
Rosefinch, Pallas's 16
Rossitten 88
Rothney Castle 34
Rothschild, Walter 82, 131
Royal Scottish Museum 87
Royal Society of London 9
Russia 5-7, 14, 20-22, 27, 74, 81, 90, 122, 124
Russian Geographical Society 21
Ruttun Pir 36

Sakhalin 26-27

Saltee 88
Salurnai, River 21
Salween 38
Samara 10
Sandgrouse, Pallas's 16
Sandwich Bay 97-98, 103
Saunders, Howard 69, 113
Scandinavia 89-90, 122-123, 129
Schrenck, Leopold von 22
Schwarz, Ludwig 21
Schwedow 26
Scilly, Isles of 100, 105
Scotland, 87
Scott, Bob 100, 121
Scott, Peter 118
Second Kamchatka Expedition 6
Second Yarkand Mission 37
Sea Eagle, Steller's 7
Seahouses 90
Second Opium War 40-41
Second War 88-89, 115
Sedimi 23
Seebohm, Henry 27, 58-60, 76, 79, 81, 89, 112
Selborne 9, 136
Selenga, River 7, 12, 25
Selenginskaja 12
Shaanxi Province 49
Shanghai 39, 46
Shantou 45
Shanxi Province 49
Sharpe, Richard Bowdler 34, 79, 112
Shaweishan Island 46
Shetland 87, 104, 124
Shilka, River 14
Shrike, Great Grey 59, 91
Shrike, Isabelline 55, 90, 102

Siberia 5, 6, 8, 10, 12-15, 20-23, 25, 27, 35, 38, 41, 47, 50, 52, 54, 56, 60-61, 75-76, 80-81, 104, 106-107, 112, 122-123, 126, 128-129, 132, 137
Sibley, Charles 138
Sichuan Province 40, 48, 132
Simla 34, 37, 131
Sind, River 35
Skokholm 88
Skolkov, Ivan 26
Smit, Joseph 111
Snipe, Great 66
Snipe, Swinhoe's 40
Snowfinch, Père David's 49
Society of Wildlife Artists 116
Sonamarg 35
Southwell, Thomas 68
Soviet Union 136
Spain 129
Spurn Point 88, 99
Srinagar 36
Staffordshire 101
Stantitza Busse 22
Stanovoy Mountains 21, 27
Steller, Georg 7, 9
Stint, Little 59
St. Agnes 100
St. Catherine's Point 100
St. Lawrence Island 127
St. Petersburg 7, 9-10, 15, 20-22, 26, 48
Stoliczka, Ferdinand 37
Stonechats 56
Strickland, Hugh 78-79
St. Kilda 87
Styan, Frederick 44-45
Suaeda 64
Suifen, River 26
Suffolk 65, 90

Sule Skerry 87
Sussex 65
Swinhoe, Robert 40-44, 71, 75
Sybiriaks 23

Taczanowski, Wladislaw 23, 25, 75
Taiwan 40, 43
Taklimakan Desert 47
Talmine Bay 107
Tarei-Nor, Lake 22
Taymyr Peninsula 21
Tbilisi 21
Tenasserim 38
Thorburn, Archibald 113-116
Thrush, Black-throated 55, 102
Thrush, Dusky 55
Thrush, Red-throated 13, 55
Thrush, Siberian 90
Thrush, White's 55, 114
Tianjin, Treaty of 40
Tian Shan Mountains 47
Ticehurst, Claud 131-132
Ticehurst, Norman 115, 131
Tibet 47-48
Tibetan Plateau 124
Tit, Blue 97
Tit, Japanese 44
Tit, Père David's 49
Tit, Silver-throated 49
Tobolsk 10
Tongzhou 43
Transbaikalia 5, 6, 22-23, 26-27, 74
Tring 82
Trusler, Rev. Dr. John 11
Tschikoi, River 12
Tucker, Bernard 115, 133
Tunniclife, Charles 116

Turkestan 37
Twite 12
Tyumen 7

Uda 12
Ural Mountains 5, 7, 10, 54
Ural, River 61, 104
Uschakovka, River 26
Ushant 87
Ussuri, River 22, 26
Ussuri Region 22, 26-27, 56
Ussuriysk 26
Uttarakhand 29, 35

Vaurie, Charles 132
Vigors, Nicholas 51
Vinicombe, Keith 126
Vitim, River 27
Vladivostok 23, 26
Volga, Lower 10
Voltaire 9

Wagtail, Citrine 90
Wallace, Ian 102-103
Walton-on-the-Naze 99
Warbler, Aquatic 59, 66
Warbler, Ashy-throated Leaf 31
Warbler, Barred 65
Warbler, Blyth's Reed 31, 87
Warbler, Brooks's Leaf 36
Warbler, Chinese Leaf 140
Warbler, Dusky 44, 54, 101-102, 112
Warbler, Eastern Crowned 56, 58
Warbler, Gansu Leaf 138
Warbler, Hume's 34, 106, 119
Warbler, Lanceolated 117
Warbler, Lemon-rumped 134, 137

Warbler, Middendorff's Grasshopper 21, 44
Warbler, Orange-barred Leaf 31
Warbler, Pallas's Grasshopper 54, 117
Warbler, Radde's 22, 101-102
Warbler, Sichuan Leaf 139
Warbler, Styan's Grasshopper 44
Warbler, Thick-billed 90
Warbler, Tytler's 36
Warbler, Willow 90, 136
Warbler, Wood 136
Warbler, Yellow-browed 21, 31, 43, 45, 54, 56, 59, 67-68, 71, 75, 87, 90, 92, 96, 101-103, 106, 112, 114, 119, 121, 124, 126-127
Warsaw 23
West Siberian Plain 10
Weston-under-Lizard 101
Wheatear, Hume's 34
Whinchat 89
White, Gilbert 9, 136
Williamson, Kenneth 88-89, 122-123, 133
Witherby, Harry 80, 82, 86, 115, 132
Wolf, Joseph 111
Wolstenholme, Peter 99
Wuhan 49
Wuyi Mountains 45

Xiamen 40-41, 43
Xian 49
Xining 132

Yablonoi Mountains 14
Yakutsk 7
Yangtze, River 40, 44, 46, 48-49
Yantai 40
Yarmouth, Great 65, 71
Yarrell, William 69
Yenisei, River 5, 7, 10, 27, 81

Yeniseysk 5, 7
Yorkshire 65, 99
Yorkshire, West 103
Yunnan Province 46, 131-132

Zarudny, Nikolai 61, 104
Zhangjiakou 48
Zhenjiang 45
Zoological Society of London 31, 51, 63, 69, 71